INSANE 1

INSANE TAXI DRIVER CONFESSIONS

by

Aaron Kline

Author: Aaron Kline
Edited by: Kinza Akbar
Typeset by: Abdassamad Clarke
Cover design by: George Davis

A catalogue record of this book is available from the British Library.

ISBN-13:   978-1-9160497-0-3 (paperback)
                     978-1-9160497-1-0 (Kindle)

Printed and bound by: Amazon

The Author

Aaron Kline is a self-employed property insurance salesman, who graduated from Law School at Staffordshire University in 1999. Two years ago, he stumbled upon a part-time opportunity to work with a popular internet-based taxi company in Leeds. Because he is a sociable person, he collated stories from passengers, fellow taxi drivers, and countless personal encounters from driving around in Yorkshire.

Acknowledgements

Many thanks to my passengers and colleagues for sharing their stories with me. The wonderful residents of Leeds have shown tremendous support and love for my idea of this book, encouraging me to publish it – until I finally did. Without them, this book may never have come into existence.

A special thanks to Jeremy Yusuf Rowland for not only proofreading this book, but for guiding me through the creative process of storytelling and always cheering me on.

I would also like to thank Kinza Akbar who deserves my gratitude for editing the book and bringing out the humour in my stories, and Abdassamad Clarke for his typesetting and advice. Thank you to my illustrator George Davis for his talented skills displayed in the unique book cover. Their assistance and expertise has shaped the book into the entertaining read it is.

Much appreciation to my wife and children for giving me time and space whilst I was writing. Their patience and respect has not only made me the author presenting this book, but also a better person in general.

Contents

The Author   v

Acknowledgements   vi

Introduction   1

My First Time   5

Lust Overpowers Love   9

The Dilemma   11

The Role Model   13

The Good Samaritan   15

The Family Affair   17

Farting Customers   19

Gruesome Halloween   22

Turtled   23

Pissing Drunk   25

The Wrong Direction   27

Bruised Black Eye   29

The Drunken Domestic 31

Rumble in the Cab 33

Abusive Couple 35

She's in Control 37

Girl at the BP Petrol Station 40

Spiked 42

Banana Woman 45

Entrapment 47

The IT Consultant 49

Rejected Ego 52

A Better Option 54

Dodgy Nightclub 56

He's not drunk 60

Suicide 63

Parental Supervision 65

The Cabbie's Son 66

Powder My Nose 68

The Student Stripper 70

Weekly Casino Budget 72

Rich Student 74

The Compensation Culture 76

Charitable Taxi Driver 79

Georgia on My Mind 81

Touchy Taxi Driver 83

The Numbers Game   85

He's in a Hurry   88

Gutters and Gutted   90

Snapchat Cabbie   92

Stalking Taxi Driver   93

The Self-Employed Physiotherapist   96

Jehovah's Witness   98

Lazy People   100

Wrong Destination   102

Pepper Spray   103

My Longest Journey   106

Budapest Rats   108

The Thief   110

Overcharged   112

Extortionate Taxi Fares   114

The Dark Hole   116

Organised Taxi Criminal Gang   119

Walking Taller   121

Cracked Up   123

Through the Wall   125

Drunk Vegans   126

Thirsty?   128

Near Death   130

Brazilian Driver   132

Road Rage	134
The Great Chase	136
He's lost the plot	138
Weird Customer	139
No Ambulance	140
Sleeping Beauty	142
The Racist Old Man	144
South African Passenger	148
Irish Robbie	150
Taxi Driver Anonymous	151
Part-time Dealer, Part-time Driver	153
The Ex-CID Passenger	154
The Bus Stop Woman	156
The Posh Guy from Harrogate	158
Abducted Driver	162
The Conspiracy Theorist	164
Street in Bloom	166
Strange Passenger	168
One Dog at a Time	171
Conclusion	173

Introduction

I am proud to say that I was born and raised in the flourishing city of Leeds, situated in the county of West Yorkshire. Leeds is considered to be the capital of Northern England, a friendly and lively place that attracts new residents, not only from all over the country, but from around the world. In fact, Leeds is ranked amongst some of the most visited places in Europe.

Given its prestigious universities, Leeds welcomes students from various disciplines. When people come here to study, they tend to stick around after their education because it is a vibrant place with plenty of opportunities. Students from Southern England enjoy living here because they embrace the warm atmosphere – although perhaps not the colder weather – that is lacking back home. People also appreciate the slower pace up North, in comparison to London for example where people aren't as communicative and instead are more isolated, curt and assertive in the city's constant hustle and bustle.

Customers from the South are always surprised at my pleasant conversation, confirming that the taxi drivers in London never speak to you. If someone tried to make conversation with a stranger, people would think that they were unusual or suspicious. But in Yorkshire, you can strike up a conversation whilst sitting next to a stranger at the bus stop, in a bar, on the street or anywhere else and it is considered normal.

With the second largest taxi office after the city of London, the demand for transport is clear. That's why I have been driving a private-hire taxi for approximately the last eighteen months. I have compiled stories from my own interesting encounters, as well as from passengers and other fellow taxi drivers. After collating enough short stories, I have written this book with the intention to share a raw representation of our society and people's daily lives.

Initially, my intention for writing this book was because I wanted to tell the world about my first-hand experiences and concerns for young teenagers, exposing the potential dangers that exist on a night out. I have witnessed the risks of getting too drunk and wanted to advise how vulnerable situations can be avoided. If I can help to save one person from being in a dangerous situation, I will have accomplished my original purpose for writing this book.

Over the course of time, this book has gradually evolved into a collection of stories from a wide spectrum, all outlining the crazy, dangerous, vile, humorous, seedy and overall interesting truths about people's real and untold experiences.

In order to respect people's privacy, I have kept the anonymity of people involved in each story. For that reason, I have changed the names, locations and sometimes even certain information that could directly indicate the people involved. The general structure and storylines are unchanged, and therefore the core fabric of each story remains unique.

The taxi vehicle itself is a small space, with four passenger seats situated close to each other. Sitting next to complete strangers in this confined space for a short amount of time gives me the opportunity to converse with people from all different walks of life. Even when a group of people are talking amongst themselves, they often welcome the driver's involvement in their conversation, which is a great opportunity for me to be sociable. With lone passengers, however, they consider you to be a short-term friend whilst they are drunk.

If a passenger doesn't want to talk, I never make any negative assumptions that they are rude. Sometimes, a silent person could be the world's nicest person who just wants to be left alone. The majority of the passengers will converse with you, and the few who don't may not want to talk because they're either too drunk, on the phone to someone else, tired or have a lot on their mind.

Working mostly evenings and nights, I tend to pick up people who are drunk or at least a bit tipsy. Either way, they let their guards down. In this state, they will confess anything – especially to a stranger. As a taxi driver, you learn about people's secret lives and they tell you things that they will never share with their spouse or family members, especially not if they were sober. You witness some interesting habits, especially when male customers, married or in relationships, tell you about the best brothels in town, as though it's normal for them to visit these places.

The taxi driver is invisible; the person everyone expects to turn a blind eye, keeping conversations within the five-door vehicle and dismissing everything mentioned once the journey is over. The fact that we carry a multitude of people to seedy locations makes passengers feel confident about their infidelity. They will unload their burden, tell you about their personal problems and justify their behaviour, all the while expecting an empathetic response about their actions. Passengers know that they probably won't ever see you again, so any information shared during a cab ride is inconsequential. This consolidates the fact that driving a cab is one of the most interesting situations: conversing with total strangers whilst they're intoxicated.

Sometimes you have to be very diplomatic, making sure that you don't express your real opinion about the passenger's actions, whether it's cheating on their partners or buying and taking drugs. Sometimes, I feel like I'm a psychotherapist, listening to people's problems and advising them to make the right decisions. You get a first-hand experience, gaining a lot of insight about what actually happens in people's personal lives – sometimes, too much insight.

I want to share this insight with you: the reader.

My First Time

It was approximately ten p.m. on a Friday night when I was sat at home in front of the TV and I decided to check online whether or not my taxi application was live. To my surprise, all of the documentation had been approved. Realising that I can now start working at any time, what was I waiting for?

I decided to immediately set off onto my new, self-employed night venture. I was excited to find out what the business was all about and headed directly to the busiest location on a Friday night: Leeds city centre, approximately two miles away from my home.

My first journey was easy. I collected a couple from outside a pub. They were too busy talking to each other, and travelled just half a mile outside of the city. They both thanked me and then hurried off, still caught up in their own chit chatter.

On my second journey, I collected a young female in her mid-thirties from a swanky bar in the centre. Surprisingly, Sarah sat next to me in the front passenger seat. She conversed about how her night was going; she was out on a work night out and left early because she wasn't feeling well. After a few minutes, she closed her eyes, perhaps for a nap I thought, so I didn't disturb her and carried on driving.

Four miles later, Sarah's eyes suddenly darted open, her face momentarily filled with panic as she looked at me. Then, she turned her face forward and violently vomited all over herself, only partially into her handbag. She was covered in it.

I immediately stopped the car in shock, reaching over to open her door so she could let out any more vomit. She managed to puke further out into the road, before she gradually came to her senses and profusely apologised about the mess she had made in the cab. She sat there helplessly whilst crying and apologising for what she had done.

Whilst I was deeply devastated for her plight, I couldn't believe what I had got myself into. Is this what I want to do for a living? Dealing with drunkards vomiting in my car on a Friday night was not what I had expected.

I was absolutely gutted. What a nightmare. But right now, I just wanted to get her home – and out of my car.

I was aware that I could take photos of the mess and email the receipts for the cleaning, but it was all an inconvenience, as well as the fact that I couldn't work for the rest of the night. After ten long minutes when she had finished vomiting, we carried on with the journey to her house. On arrival, I asked her if she could get me some wipes and cleaning detergent to try and reduce the smell in the vehicle, before I retire back home to my TV for the rest of the night and contemplate this amazing career opportunity.

To my surprise, when she got out of the car, I saw that she had only vomited on herself and in her handbag. I couldn't believe my luck. The seat had a small wet patch, which I managed to easily clean when her husband came rushing out with wet wipes and dry towels. I gave the seat a full wipe down which helped get rid of the smell in the car. I thought she had made a real mess over the seat and floor, but it was all clear, so I was good to carry on with the rest of the shift.

Her husband was fuming about how she cannot handle her drink and always manages to vomit when she's drunk. I assured him that my car was fine, so I wouldn't be claiming for any extra cleaning costs. I also asked him for some carrier bags to store away in the glove compartment, just in case anyone else treated me to their alcohol-infused vomit during the rest of the night.

As I left, I was still very upset that despite her seeming like such an intelligent person, she couldn't even tell me to pull over in time. Instead, she carelessly risked a mess inside the vehicle. She didn't admit she was feeling sick because she was embarrassed, which had come at the cost of her vomiting all over herself with a complete lack of regard for myself. After this experience, I decided that if I ever had a customer who was too drunk then I simply wouldn't let them ride with me.

Glad to move on from this disgusting situation, I drove back towards the city for the next challenge. As I was driving, I heard a mobile phone ringing from underneath the passenger seat. I pulled over, retrieving the phone from under the car seat with dread. It was Sarah's husband calling her phone. The call must have been for me to return her phone.

I had driven about three miles away from her house and had enough of her nonsense tonight. I was not going to travel back to her house on a busy Friday night, missing out on even more customers. Instead, I handed it into the taxi office on Monday morning, so she could drive down to the office and collect it herself.

Well, I thought to myself, that's karma.

Lust Overpowers Love

It was approximately two a.m. in the town centre when my passenger got into the front seat of the car. I asked him to confirm where he was going, but in response he defensively asked if I was being funny with him.

Confused about his hostility, I told him I just wanted to make sure that he entered his destination correctly on the taxi phone app as people often make a mistake. He apologised for his initial comment and confirmed that he was attending a well-known massage parlour that was two miles outside of the city centre.

I realised that he thought I was being funny with him because he was going to a brothel. I clarified that internet-based taxi drivers don't know where a customer is going until the passenger gets into the car and the route begins on the app.

Whilst we headed to the brothel, the customer was frustratedly scrolling through his phone, so I asked if everything was alright. He told me that he shared the same iCloud with his wife and so she'd be able to see his exact location and his duration in that place.

Even though she wouldn't know it was a brothel, she would want to know what he was doing at that particular location for three hours on a Wednesday at two o'clock in the morning. I warned that he was taking quite a risk by jeopardising his marriage, but he wasn't interested in my advice since lust is an overwhelming feeling. She was on a night shift as a nurse in York, so he was hoping that she wouldn't find time to check up on him.

This guy was prepared to risk everything for a night at the brothel, bragging about how rich he was as a successful broker. He kindly tipped me ten pounds too, as a testimony of his wealth.

One night, I received a job to collect a middle-aged man from a hotel at roughly one a.m. As we got talking, I noticed his Russian accent and he told me that he was a director in a European company and that they have business interests here in the U.K. He was a pleasant gentleman, sharing that he was happily married and that they had three children. His family was in Russia whilst he was branching out on a business trip.

However, the reason he was in the car with me was because he was on his way to the local brothel. Obviously he hadn't told me this, but I realised when I dropped him off.

I realise just how naïve I am, since I would never expect a person of this calibre to go to the seedy side of town. These encounters have shown that although these types of people will claim to be content in their marriage and family life, they will never be fully satisfied. They succumb to lust, which unfortunately overpowers their 'love'.

The Dilemma

On an early Sunday morning following a Saturday night, I was travelling back to Leeds from York when a job alert came up for a small village that was conveniently nearby. I picked up a drunk and distressed couple in their late thirties, now heading back to York. They were conversing about a very sticky situation of theirs.

The story unfolded as I listened attentively. They were discussing where they were going, which was apparently the man's house. Only thing was, his wife was there. She was waiting for him to explain what he was doing on a night out with this woman.

Someone had spotted them together and notified his wife. This man, a husband and a father, had told his wife that he was out with some work colleagues. The wife called him to tell him that she would set his clothes on fire, along with his work laptop, if he didn't come home as soon as possible along with the woman that he had been with.

During the journey, they were discussing who could have notified his wife. The dilemma was that they weren't sure if anyone had spotted them being intimate during the night. Their plan was to wait and see how much his wife actually knew, and then deal with it accordingly. Since this woman was a work colleague as well, it created the perfect alibi.

The man was really shaken by the whole situation. He kept placing his hands on his head, trying to comprehend the reality of what would happen when he got to the house. His furious wife was waiting to dissect him into small pieces.

I was in awe of his wife's genius threat of burning her husband's items which forced him to bring the other woman home as well. I feel she would be too cunning for whatever lie these two drunken fools were cooking up. On arrival, I wished I could have been a fly on the wall to see the wife launch her attack.

The Role Model

John told me a story about when he got a taxi to the hospital as his wife had just had their first child. The car was in a real state, with a vile smell and lots of dog hair on the back seat. The driver said he has three dogs and forgot to clean the back of the car. I wonder how many of his customers hear this excuse on a daily basis.

Whilst on the journey, the cabbie congratulated John on becoming a father. He told John that he had four children himself, with the eldest being thirteen years old. The driver expressed how great it is to be married and have a big family, especially watching your children grow up and develop their own personalities. Despite the lack of cleanliness in the car, the cabbie seemed to be a loving family man.

A little later in the journey, they were driving past rows of local shops when the cabbie pointed at the upstairs of one of the shops and informed John that it was a brothel. The cabbie began talking about the quality of women in the different brothels around the city, and he even recommended which ones had the best value. He told John to mention his name, to make sure he received the best service.

John was taken back at the sudden change of topic. He couldn't believe the cabbie was talking about different brothels with the same enthusiasm and passion as when he was talking about his family earlier.

Some people do not have any guilty conscience at all. Partly as a personal vendetta against him, John decided to lodge a complaint to the taxi company about the rotten smell and dirtiness of the cab.

The Good Samaritan

Around Christmas time, I was taking a couple home after their festive office party. For the entire journey of thirty minutes, they were very intimate and couldn't keep their hands off each other. When I arrived at the house, she insisted that Martin come in with her. However, he was adamant that he wanted to carry on with his journey home, for whatever reason.

This went on for a few minutes as she tried to convince him to stay for an hour, offering to pay for his taxi home later, but he just wasn't giving in. Eventually, she gave up and allowed him to make his way home.

As I was dropping Martin off, he began to tell me how she was just a colleague from work that was going through a divorce. She had been feeling lonely, depressed and just wanted a bit of attention. But he couldn't stay with her as he had to go home to his wife and children since he was an honest and loyal man.

I was slightly confused at how he reached that conclusion. Martin had snogged his work colleague for half an hour, but at least he wasn't going to have sex with her.

It seemed Martin was quite proud of himself for going home to his wife and kids. I don't know if his wife would share this sense of achievement. Regardless, he had apparently been a 'good Samaritan' to his colleague and at least made her feel better. I wonder if he's allowed to add this to his next appraisal meeting at work.

The Family Affair

One cabbie told me about the time he collected a couple of guys from a gay bar. They were very intimate in the back seats, touching and kissing each other. The cabbie overheard their conversation as they talked about their experiences with other men. He assumed that these guys were in an open relationship and even comfortable enough to discuss these affairs. He dropped them off to a house where they apparently lived together as a couple too.

A few weeks later, and by coincidence, the same cabbie collected someone else from that same house. On this occasion, the couple were waiting outside with their friend that was getting into the taxi. They recognised it was the same driver that had dropped them off a few weeks back and greeted him.

When their friend got into the taxi, the driver initiated the conversation about dropping the couple off at this house a few weeks ago. The passenger told the driver that they were not a couple, but brothers. When the driver heard this, he was shocked into disbelief. He asked for confirmation and shared his understanding that they were lovers.

"They are both gay, but they're brothers. They're not lovers at all."

The cabbie was confused about what he had been told. He explained to the passenger that when they were in his taxi, they were being extremely affectionate with each other. The passenger refused to acknowledge this information, claiming it wasn't possible because he'd known the brothers for years and they do not have an incestuous relationship. He was adamant that there was nothing going on between the brothers and that there must have been a misunderstanding. The driver insisted that he knew the difference between a peck on the cheek and a French kiss. At this point, the passenger took a deep breath and fell into silence.

The driver regretted mentioning anything to the passenger as it could create drama in their personal lives. The passenger could've even been in a relationship with one of the brothers. But it was too late and there was no taking back this disturbing information. The passenger remained quiet and the rest of the trip was tense. On arrival, the passenger didn't say a word as he left the taxi, slamming the door shut.

Unfortunately, taxi drivers don't know what happens in the customer's life after that door shuts.

Farting Customers

A male farting in a taxi is a completely different experience compared to a female doing the same. If a male farts, then he will either forewarn you or confess to it straight away. They avoid embarrassment by clearing the air – and take pleasure in polluting it.

In fact, if there is a group of guys in the cab and one of them farts, then he will probably do his best to make it as loud as possible with the hope that the smell is poignant. It's all part of their boyish and crude humour, including the verbally abusive response of the drunken friends. To be honest, even if they don't need to fart they'll force one out for the banter. Some men grow old, but they never grow up.

However, it's totally taboo if a woman farts, as if they aren't also human beings with a functional body. Women are assumed to have more self-restraint, making it very rare that one would let one rip in company. But alas, accidents happen.

On a winter's afternoon, a girl sat next to me in the front

passenger seat. Early on in the journey, she silently farted. The smell got around the car very quickly due to it being a small space, and with the windows closed and the heaters circulating air around the car, it didn't take long for my nostrils to latch onto her wonderful odour.

I desperately wanted to open the windows, but my chivalrous self was concerned that it would bring attention to her accident and she would feel embarrassed. Obviously, she would know why I suddenly wound the car window down in cold weather. It's difficult when there's an obvious culprit.

To save face and create a distraction from the odour, she kept talking for a long time. We had approximately half a mile left to travel and at this point, I didn't have a clue what she was talking about because the smell had grasped my attention. During the longest half mile of my life, I drove as fast as I could and had never felt so relieved on arrival.

As soon as I pulled up outside her house, I told her it was a pleasure and she bolted out of the car, hurriedly saying goodbye. This had to be the most awkward moment in my taxi career. I simply didn't know how to react. I hoped I would get five stars for my patience though, and I can only pray that I don't get another lone female farter in the car.

One night, I had four girls in the cab when one of them farted. There was no chance that anyone was going to admit that one. Instead, the farter's pride resulted in the whole group quarrelling for the rest of the way to the hotel. I was just thankful that this time I could at least put the windows down straight away and get rid of the odour without offending anyone, and instead having a laugh about it.

A friend of mine once told me that he has been married for three years and his wife had never farted in his presence. I asked him what else she could be hiding from him. That made him paranoid, for sure.

The only thing that can sometimes be worse than the smell of farts is bad breath. When faced with customers with particularly offensive smells, I take a mint for myself and then offer the customer one, with hope that they accept my subtle gesture. It works out well as the rest of the journey becomes refreshing as opposed to painful. However, not all customers will have one and if the passenger sat next to you is a chatty drunkard, then you're in for a real treat.

Gruesome Halloween

My taxi driver friend collected a group of army officers after they had been clubbing in Leeds on Halloween. They wanted to travel back to their army barracks in North Yorkshire, which was approximately fifty miles away. On the way, one of the guys needed to puke up. This was somewhat unleashed onto his clothes, but luckily the rest of it was projected outside of the car.

Whilst he was puking up, he decided he also needed to relieve himself for a number two. Since he didn't have any toilet paper to wipe off the excess, he handled the situation with machismo; he pulled up his pants and jumped straight back into the car.

After this, the soldiers fell asleep, too drunk to be bothered about the smell of fresh shit and puke. But the sober taxi driver certainly felt the brunt of the lethal cocktail combo, gracing his nose all the way to their army barracks.

He described the smell as the vilest smell that someone could ever experience, and he was sat in a confined space with it. Soldiers *are* used to worse conditions though.

Turtled

On a quiet Sunday night in the middle of winter, I received a job to collect someone from Leeds city centre. Lauren was waiting outside in the cold, with her suitcase by her side and dressed in her pyjamas. Something was off. When she got into the back of the cab, I realised she was very upset and asked her if everything was alright. She tried to assure me that she was alright, but it was hard to believe whilst she was blowing her nose and crying at the same time.

As the journey commenced, I asked out of curiosity why she was travelling in her pyjamas in the cold. She told me that she had fallen out with her boyfriend because of his disgusting behaviour. Apparently, she'd had enough of his stupidity and after their argument, decided to go to her friend's place. Sounds like a typical domestic gone too far.

When passengers are upset, I usually stay quiet unless the person is up for sharing. In this case Lauren wanted to tell me about the dispute with her boyfriend. As stupid as it sounds, she said, her boyfriend had turtled her too many times after repeatedly being warned that it's not funny anymore. He still finds it hilarious, but she has to go to work in the morning and his antics disturb her.

I was confused. What the hell is turtling?

She described that when she is lying in bed, her boyfriend covers her with the bed sheets and then farts. This traps the fart, forcing her to wake up due to the revolting odour, and then he keeps her under the sheets to appreciate the smell for longer.

Apparently, she'd been turtled.

This is a terrible prank to even play once, but behaving like this when she has work in the morning is beyond idiocy. He had been warned to stop, and now it has ended in a bitter row. She had been forced to pack her bags and leave in the early hours of the morning.

One turtle too many.

Pissing Drunk

A passenger once told me that his sister-in-law couldn't handle alcohol at all. She would just piss herself whilst walking down the street on a night out. She's even unloaded her bowels in a taxi once and ended up at the police station because she refused to pay the fine. Some people should not be drinking, or rather, they shouldn't be allowed out at all.

One fellow cabbie took the risk and picked up a very drunk lady on a busy weekend night, mainly because of the attractive 3.6x surge on the fare. During the five-mile journey, the driver smelled a fart and so he immediately wound down the car windows. The passenger was blissfully passed out in the rear.

Unfortunately, even with the windows down, the smell lingered. Upon arrival, the driver gets out of the taxi to wake the customer, only to realise that the persistent smell was because she had soiled herself and the back seats of the car.

She wasn't in any state to show remorse about her revolting accident. However, he did manage to salvage thirty-five pounds towards the cleaning costs. The cabbie shot to the nearest twenty-four-hour petrol station and thoroughly cleaned the soiled PVC seats with tissues and wipes. After cleaning the poop, he was able to carry on working for the rest of the night.

Although he was given thirty-five pounds for the mess, the driver also attempted to claim another one hundred and fifty pounds by uploading photos of the accident on the phone app. She put up a real fight with the taxi firm, arguing that she had already paid a charge, so he only recovered another twenty pounds.

It's fair to say that he probably did deserve more money for the emotional distress of cleaning another person's shit!

The Wrong Direction

As a taxi driver I'm beginning to learn that the more drunk one gets, the more the world looks like a personal urinal. Some people will 'crack on' in the middle of the pavement or the road. Apparently, any lamppost or wall will lead them to believe that they're in a secluded location, leaving the sober half of us to witness some ungodly sights.

One taxi driver had a drunken customer that desperately needed to empty his bladder, so he pulled up to a lay-by on the side of a country road. The passenger began urinating, but in his drunken state he didn't realise he was swaying around and had changed direction to face the taxi. With his eyes closed, he was urinating on the side of the taxi, pissing directly onto the back seats.

The driver was too late to realise, and when he did there was already a gallon of urine on the seats and floor. This had quickly turned into any taxi driver's worst nightmare. He jumped out of the cab to stop the drunken man, who was too busy taking pleasure in urinating that he was totally oblivious of his actions.

The driver shot around the car and moved him away from the car, accidentally tripping the drunkard onto the pavement. Although the man was now on the ground, he was still peeing away, now onto the driver's trousers too.

The driver, of course, became even more furious, and didn't want to leave until he was given money for this mess. He collected forty-five pounds from the customer, which still wasn't enough to clean a gallon of urine inside the car, but it was better than nothing. He drove off, leaving the guy in a puddle of his urine, but with an empty bladder at least.

Bruised Black Eye

I was collecting passengers from the city centre on a standard Friday night shift, when two men got into my car early Saturday morning. I turned around to greet the customers and couldn't help but notice that one had a badly bruised right eye, which lead the conversation on the journey.

James and Stephen were out on a work night out in one of the busier areas of town. In one of the bars they were in, there was a boisterous couple arguing. People became aware of the argument that was occurring and the growing rage between the couple made the situation look quite tense.

Suddenly, the guy punched the girl directly in the face, dropping her unconscious. Several people quickly went over to help the girl, whilst James and some other guys ran over to restrain the woman-beater before he inflicted any more damage. They chased him out of the bar and down the street, following him into a hotel's restaurant where this bloke went berserk. He started throwing plates at the group of guys to prevent them from catching him.

Bravely, James confronted him head-on, but was instantly smacked in his left eye and fell to the ground. Stephen's intervention saved the day as he dived in and managed to pin the abuser to the ground. The other guys got a chance to throw some punches in too whilst they waited for the police to arrive.

The restaurant was in a real mess with broken cutlery thrown all over the place. The hotel staff were standing there in shock as they watched the whole scene play out. Eventually, an hour and a half later, the police arrived and arrested the drunkard. They shook hands with the guys, thanking them for their heroic efforts.

The guys stuck around at the hotel bar to have a few drinks, courtesy of the kind hotel manager, as they had to give a statement to the police about the whole encounter. Four hours later, their Friday night was over, wasted on chasing some abusive idiot around town. Not all superheroes wear capes.

The Drunken Domestic

Alan got into my car on a Saturday night, along with his sister and his girlfriend. Before they even got into the car, they were at each other's throats in a heated argument. The story unfolds about Alan's sister's boyfriend Terrence, who was with them in one of the bars in town earlier.

Talking and drinking amongst themselves, Terence foolishly said to Alan that his sister was a slag, complaining that he's fed up with everything. Of course, Alan didn't like this comment about his sister. He reacted in rage, punching Terrence in the face and leaving him unconscious on the floor.

Funnily enough, the sister was upset that Alan had punched her boyfriend. She felt that he should have just informed her about this, leaving it for her to decide what action she felt was appropriate.

Alan's argument was that Terence had made an abusive comment about his sister, which he believed deserved a smack to protect their family honour. He was unable to control his anger and felt it was his duty as a brother to give Terence his best right hook and take the mouthy culprit down instantly.

Alan wanted my opinion on the matter and I agreed that Terence should not have made the disrespectful remark about Alan's sister, especially not to the brother. I said that Alan may have overreacted by hitting Terence, but his anger was justified and therefore his reaction would have been instinctive.

The sister probably didn't want to jeopardise her entire relationship with Terence, shaky as it may be. Perhaps she just wanted to forgive him and move on quickly, but it will be a bit trickier to patch things up now that Terence has a broken jaw.

When people are drunk, their real thoughts and feelings are revealed, and this story is a prime example of why drunken honesty is not always a good idea.

Rumble in the Cab

Drunk and sensitive at four a.m., three student girls began arguing in a taxi. The argument began because Sam was dragged away in the middle of a conversation with some guy. Apparently, her friend Emma, who was sat in the front seat, had interfered on several different occasions whilst Sam has been talking to a bloke.

Sam accused Emma of being jealous, ranting that she didn't need her to dictate who she speaks to, because nobody should interfere in her personal life. The argument got really heated, and something Sam said in anger touched a nerve with Emma.

In a sudden rage, Emma turned around and started slapping and punching Sam, telling her to shut the fuck up. Sam retaliated by booting Emma in the face, causing her lip to split open and bleed. Emma fought back, and before long they were both screaming and shouting, pulling at each other's hair like wildcats.

The driver parked up because the situation had escalated

tremendously. He pulled Emma back down into the front seat and warned the girls that they would have to leave the car if they carried on fighting. There was still another five miles to the journey and he wasn't going to tolerate this kind of behaviour for the rest of it.

The third girl helped calm the situation down with Sam in the back, whilst the driver made sure Emma had her seat belt on in the front. Frankly, he didn't want to get rid of the passengers since there was a 2.7x surge on this journey.

It looks like Emma had managed to get a real kick in the face. This fight would definitely resume when the girls got out of the car. However, they remained quiet for the rest of the journey, swallowing their pride instead of waiting for another cab in the cold.

After he had dropped them off, the cabbie wiped down the seats with their blood. Whilst cleaning up, he found one of their fake eyelashes covered in blood – a true marker of a cat fight!

Abusive Couple

In the early hours of the morning, a couple got into a taxi after a Saturday night out. They were in the middle of a domestic that started long before they got into the car and carried on throughout the journey. The guy kept on grabbing the girl by her throat, telling her to keep her mouth shut. The girl wasn't backing down, getting louder and more abusive.

As the guy grabbed the girl's throat again, this time he also slapped her sharply. This finally alerted the driver to intervene and he immediately stopped the vehicle. He opened the back-passenger door and told the male to stop hitting her otherwise he would have to leave the car. The woman immediately spoke up in defence of her boyfriend, yelling at the driver instead.

"Mind your own fucking business and get on with the journey!"

The driver was stumped at this unexpected response, feeling like an idiot for trying to do the right thing by preventing the boyfriend from abusing the girl. He jumped straight back into the cab and drove on, ignoring the wildly abusive couple.

Unfortunately, women can be just as abusive to men as well. It was early evening when a couple arrived, dressed nicely to go out. The lady opened the back door and got into the vehicle, before the man asked her to shuffle up so he could get in as well.

"How dare you tell me to shuffle up? You should have had the courtesy to open the door for me, never mind shuffle me up! You can go around the other side."

Deadbeat, he closed her door shut and walked around the side to get in whilst she called him a "stupid fucking moron."At first, I thought she was just joking at first, but no – she was horrendously offended.

The man tried to hide his embarrassment, nonchalantly telling her that it wasn't a big deal. But he was only digging a bigger hole.

"Didn't your mother teach you any manners? I'm sorry but these are basic rules that should be followed!"

There's etiquette, there's high-maintenance, but then... there's abusive.

She's in Control

As always, it was a busy student night in Leeds. I collected a young couple from outside a nightclub at approximately half past four in the morning. The sky was getting pretty light and I wanted to get home, making this my last journey. The passengers requested to go to Moortown, which is about four miles out of the city.

On the way there, the couple were very passionately cuddling and kissing in the back and I assumed they were in a relationship. That was until we arrived at the destination and the girl refused to leave the car, telling the man that she wants to go home. He was holding her by the hand and trying to pull her out of the taxi, commencing a tug of war. She insisted that she wanted to be dropped off home.

This ride was on her account, so I had no issue with her staying in the car and taking her wherever she wanted. After five painful minutes of watching the desperate guy try to pressurize her, he started trying to pull her out of the car. At this point, I intervened because the girl was getting upset and needed some support. I told the guy that if she doesn't want to go with him, he should leave her alone. Finally, he backed down, but he was still furious as he swore at her. He walked away alone without the lady, but life is such sometimes.

Afterwards when I was heading to her destination, I realised she lives in student halls. She was in her first year at university and had just turned eighteen. It was also her first time away from her home in Manchester. I asked her what she was doing with the guy who was forcing her to go home with him.

Apparently, she met this bloke outside the club and he wanted a lift home. She was kind enough, or should I say naive enough, to let him add his address on her phone application to take a taxi together. All this happened within five minutes of meeting this total stranger outside the club.

This local guy must have noticed the young and vulnerable student standing outside on her own and tried to take advantage of the situation. Luckily for her, I got rid of him. Perhaps if it was another taxi driver that wasn't as bothered, he would have told them both to get out of the car which would've left her in a dangerous situation.

Although she insisted that she was in control of the situation, from my perspective she could have easily been taken advantage of. I told her that no matter how smart and in control she thinks she is, the guy had managed to arrange a taxi with her. I advised that she should always make sure she is accompanied with a friend when she's out, just in case she gets too intoxicated to the point of not knowing what she is doing.

She was eighteen years old and had spent her life at home

under parental supervision. All of a sudden, she moved to a large metropolitan city to study, and had no real life experience to draw upon. Many in similar situations are taken advantage of, or, in some horrific cases, sexually abused.

Girl at the BP Petrol Station

Back in early May, I finished a shift at five a.m. and went to the local BP petrol station to refuel for the next day. As I walked into the shop to pay for the fuel, I couldn't help but notice a young girl sat on a stool crying and in a very bad state.

I asked the worker what was going on, only to find out that she was a local student who had been followed out of a pub by two guys and then lured into their car where she was raped.

She had bite marks all over her neck and her shirt buttons were torn. She was dressed like she had been on a night out, holding her heels in one hand and clutching her torn shirt together with the other. Her face was very pale and tears were continually streaming down her face. Although she was very drunk during the encounter, she managed to get away and ran into the petrol station for help. The staff notified the police whilst she waited in the shop.

I was deeply saddened about this incident and wanted to speak to her, but she had already explained everything to the staff at the petrol station and I'm sure the police will be speaking to her until morning, so I left her alone.

If you're a young woman, make sure that you take certain precautions when on a night out. As a taxi driver, I work nights and always see young women that are heavily intoxicated but alone. Unfortunately, there are some vile men who take advantage of these vulnerable states. But there is strength in numbers, so make sure you are accompanied by friends throughout the night.

Spiked

There is a growing concern about people's drinks getting spiked whilst out in bars and clubs. I hear stories all the time and it seems to happen to anyone and everyone; there isn't a particular age group that's targeted. It's a tragic experience to suffer, in which people completely lose control of their senses and black out until the next day.

There was one story in particular that I don't think I could ever forget, about a passenger called Nigel. Nigel told me about his experience of being spiked whilst he was backpacking in Australia for a year.

He worked in a farm for a while and moved around several bars whilst travelling. During his time in Sydney, he moved from one hostel to another as it worked out to be cheaper than renting an apartment in the bustling city. As a single care free male, he was simply enjoying his time on the other side of the world and wasn't really bothered about high standards.

On one occasion, he shared his hostel room with some friends he met whilst working in one of the bars. Simon and Zack were also from England and were travelling around Australia just like Nigel. They worked and stayed together for three weeks, and in that short time they bonded quite easily.

Sometimes after work, they would stay behind at the bar for some drinks before going back to the hostel. On one occasion, Nigel was with Simon and Zack and their colleagues Sarah and Becky having a couple of drinks. However, when he woke up the next day, he felt extremely lethargic. He woke up late into the afternoon with a heavy head, struggling to move his body or even open his eyes, and he couldn't remember anything from the night before. He also had peculiar pain in his backside, which he ignored as he tried to remedy his migraine first.

At first, he couldn't understand why he felt this way as he had barely drank, and then realised his drink must have been spiked. There could be no other explanation for his plight after just a few drinks. Later in the day, Nigel tried to go to the toilet and realised that his butthole was very sore. He didn't have a clue what could've happened for his rear area to be in so much pain and decided to go to the hospital.

The hospital examined him and said that it looked very sore and that it was possible that there may have been some penetration. Nigel was horrified as he considered the very real possibility that he had been anally raped whilst unconscious. There was no doubt something had happened, but who was responsible?

Nigel became justifiably paranoid and didn't know how to resolve the mystery. It's not like he could ask them, "who penetrated me last night?" After giving it some thought he decided to say absolutely nothing about the night and leave quickly and quietly. He went and packed his belongings and then disappeared off to a different location. He simply didn't know who to trust anymore and didn't want to risk anything happening to him again.

Over the next two weeks, Sarah and Becky called Nigel repeatedly as they were worried why he had left so quickly. On the other hand, Simon and Zack didn't show any concern whatsoever.

Maybe they knew why Nigel left.

It's safe to say that Nigel hasn't shared hostel rooms again.

Banana Woman

I collected Lauren from her university's student union building one night after she had been on a pub crawl during the day in her banana outfit. Her friend had booked the journey for me to take her home because she'd had too much to drink. Since the journey was only half a mile away and Lauren didn't seem to be in a terrible state, I decided to take the risk and drop her off quickly.

Once in the car she began to plead with me to stop at a local Hyde Park takeaway because she was famished, so I agreed. When she got out of the car and made her way to the takeaway, I noticed she was holding onto the pavement railings for support and realised how drunk she really was. I regretted accepting her request as I should have taken her straight home.

After waiting for ten minutes, I decided to go and look inside. I found Lauren slouching on the chair, blissfully asleep and snoring. Her food was on the table and there were mushy peas all over her face and banana outfit.

I didn't know what to do because if anything happened to her, I would have to explain to Lauren's friend who had booked the journey on her account. Although I felt bad leaving this girl here, I also couldn't carry her into the car because then I would have to make physical contact.

By some miracle, three girls that knew Lauren walked into the shop just then. I asked them if they would kindly help me take Lauren home since they also lived in the next street, and they gladly agreed.

I watched them carry the pea-stained banana into her house. They opened her door and placed her in the hallway, and then locked the door behind her and posted the keys through the letterbox. No doubt, she will be lying in that hallway until later the next day. But at least when she wakes up, she will have her chips and mushy peas container next to her for breakfast.

Entrapment

One Sunday morning, I collected a couple from what I understood to be their home. During the journey, I was asked to make a stop to drop the lady off at an impressively large, detached house. Leon stayed in the car and travelled another seven miles towards the city, where he had left his car the night before due to being overly intoxicated.

Leon was a chatty person and told me all about his relationship with the girl in the car, who was his girlfriend from Thailand. She was in the UK on a work permit as a maid for a rich couple, who owned the grand house from earlier. We had dropped her off so that she could clean the house ready before the family got up.

Leon had been with her for over a year, and although she wanted to get married and have children, he wasn't interested. He confided in me that he was just playing along and making false promises to keep her on the side. He only had to see her once a week because of her demanding job as a maid. Leon also told me that he already had his vasectomy done after his two kids from his first wife and had no intention of having any more children.

He believed that his girlfriend only wanted to marry him so she could apply for a British passport and stay and work in the UK. Before he met her, he was aware that she was having an affair with her employer, as the husband was a friend of a friend. Leon pretended that he didn't know about this to her. On one occasion, she had told Leon about her affair with the husband's wife, who made her get high on cocaine before sleeping together whilst the husband was abroad on business.

It seemed like she was just trying to keep the couple happy since she is vulnerable and in a different and alienating country. She was probably also worried that she would lose her job if she didn't do what they wanted. That would result in her going back to Thailand, a country that is poorer with fewer opportunities.

Although Leon was talking about the situation as if it was a joke, I could see that she was trapped in a vicious circle between the husband, the wife and Leon who were all taking advantage of her. She placed her hopes on Leon who seemed to be exploiting her for his own entertainment.

This exemplifies how someone that is desperate will try to find any way out of their situation just to become comfortable in life.

The IT Consultant

One late evening, I collected a young professional couple from outside a bar in town to take back home. The girl was very quiet, deliberately looking away from her boyfriend which gave the impression that she wasn't happy about something and they had, had a disagreement. In contrast, Ben's behaviour was very confident as he chatted away with the regular taxi conversation topics.

A little while afterwards, Ben directed his attention back to his partner and apologised for cutting the night short. He promised to her that he would make it up another time, but she totally ignored him. He continued relentlessly, explaining that he's not sure how long something will take as it may just be a minor issue and he should be back home within the hour. She still wasn't interested. I realised that he had to go somewhere in a hurry and spoiled his partner's night by taking her home early.

On arrival, Ben asked me to wait for him as he needed to travel to another destination. They both got out of the car as he attempted to walk his girlfriend to the front door. However, she stormed off and he was left following behind, desperately trying to sweeten her up one last time, but she wasn't having any of it.

After a few minutes, Ben ran back to the car and got into the front seat. He took a deep breath before complaining about getting tired of her stroppy attitude and that she was too much hard work. I could tell that he wanted my sympathy, but I didn't know her or the full story so I didn't want to agree with him for the sake of it. At the same time, however, I had to say something to keep the conversation going.

"I'm sure you'll work something out, you seem smart enough."

He replied with a very smug smirk on his face, as if to taunt me "you don't even know the half of it."

"I think I already have, mate."

He told me where he was headed now, and at this point in my taxi career I should've guessed. Apparently Ben works as a freelance IT consultant, so he takes calls at any time and often receives emergency out-of-hours jobs. Using this as an excuse to his girlfriend, he was in fact going to see another girl he met through work.

I was shocked. He was ditching his girlfriend to go see someone else and still had the audacity to complain about her always being grumpy. Maybe if he was loyal and invested time into their relationship, she wouldn't have reason to complain. I think it was pretty obvious that Ben was a selfish boy, only concerned about what he wants – which in this case was all of the cake, all for himself.

This was probably the only time in my life when I had to fight the strong temptation to go back to his house and tell his girlfriend where he was. But my job ends after the passenger leaves the car. I just hope she realises soon and gets rid of him.

Rejected Ego

Natalie's night ended pretty early as it was only midnight when I picked her up outside a very busy club, which still had a long queue at the entrance. She seemed disgruntled with some of the guys stood there, swearing at them whilst getting in to the back of the cab. She told me that whenever she rejects a guy, they can't handle it and so they hurl insults at her instead.

Earlier on in the night, she was approached by a guy in the club. After telling him she wasn't interested and wanted to be left alone, he continued to pester her by following her around for the rest of the night. To begin with, she just tried to ignore him, hoping he would give up so she could enjoy the rest of her night after paying a lot of money to get into the club in the first place.

But this guy wouldn't take no for an answer. Eventually, he began making disrespectful remarks by telling her that she was arrogant and actually wasn't even all that??????. Natalie couldn't take being tormented by this bully all night, so she decided to get a taxi home. Obviously she had dented his ego by her rejection, so in return he wanted to humiliate and belittle her to feel better about himself. He was that insecure.

I had a similar encounter with a Chinese customer who also left the club early because some guy followed her around, telling her he likes mixed race children and suggesting that she would be the ideal candidate for his future. Although she had told the doorman about the comments, he laughed it off dismissively saying that there was nothing wrong with what he was saying. He told her that she should stop over exaggerating and leave him alone. To her surprise, and mine after hearing this, the bouncer had treated her as though she was the problem.

Clearly, harassment is not taken seriously enough.

A Better Option

Gay bars have become really popular over the years. Girls seem to feel much more comfortable in a gay bar as they don't have to worry about getting groped by perverts throughout the night. They can enjoy a fun night with their friends without being harassed.

On Christmas Eve, I received a job from outside a popular gay bar in Leeds city centre. As I approached the club, there were four police vehicles parked outside the entrance and a large crowd standing outside around a bloke laying on the floor. He was unconscious and had clearly been beaten up badly, with blood all over his face. As soon as I pulled up, Tony and Sarah came out of the crowd and jumped into the car, asking me to quickly drive away from the scene.

As we drove, the couple told me about what had happened back at the club. They decided to go out to the gay joint as they always have a great time there. Whilst in the club, a bloke approached Sarah and offered to buy her a drink. Since it was the festive season, Tony appreciated the kind gesture towards his girlfriend and thought it was harmless as she was stood with him anyway.

The drunk bloke began conversing with Sarah with friendly small talk. Then, he placed his hands down her back and made his way further down to grab her bum. Sarah instinctively moved away, but he quickly grabbed her waist and pulled her closer whilst force fully kissing her neck. Sarah was panicking, yelling and screaming at him to get off whilst trying to push him away. The bloke lost his temper and snatched the drink back off her, but not before giving her a hard slap across the face.

Her boyfriend Tony and a few other guys in the bar pounced on him, beating him to the ground. He was a huge guy, apparently six foot with a muscular build, hence why he managed to pull himself up each time. He forced his way outside of the bar where he was jumped again. This time he was beaten to the ground and the guys stamped on his head whilst he was down. It had turned into a real nasty fight.

The bouncers had alerted the police as this had gone way beyond their control. When I had arrived, the cops were trying to work out what had happened. Luckily, I was the getaway car and the couple managed to avoid spending Christmas Eve at the police station writing reports. There could have even been prosecution for Tony because of the excessive force used on the bloke.

Later that night when I drove past the club, I saw that the police had closed it for the rest of the night.

Not even gay clubs are safe for girls anymore.

Dodgy Nightclub

This one night I dropped off a passenger to Huddersfield, approximately twenty miles from Leeds. The internet-based taxi firm allows you to programme the system so that you receive potential customers as you drive back towards your destination.

On the way back to Leeds, I got lucky and collected a couple from a small town called Mirfield. The girl looked very drunk and exhausted, falling asleep as soon as she got into the car. Although they'd been on a night out, the male was lively and didn't seem like he'd had anything to drink at all.

Instinctively upon sight of a drunken customer, I took a plastic bag out of the glove compartment and handed it over to the guy in case his girlfriend needed to vomit at any point. Connor assured me that she wouldn't be waking up as he believes she was spiked at the nightclub.

The couple were out in Huddersfield when his girlfriend became very drunk after the second drink, to the point that she couldn't stand up straight. He immediately realised that something wasn't right since his girlfriend never got drunk this quickly and became very worried and confused as he looked for somewhere to sit her down. Whilst he tried to decide what to do, someone barged into him and incited a fight. The bouncers intervened and dragged Connor out of the club.

Connor became outraged as his girlfriend was still in the club and he was worried about her vulnerable state. He begged the bouncers to let him in so he could get his girlfriend and go home, but the bouncers completely ignored him and his situation. There were six thuggish security guards standing outside, ready to beat him up if he tried anything, making him very anxious and helpless.

Luckily, his girlfriend had somehow managed to walk out of the club. Connor quickly got her into the first taxi he could find and headed back home to Leeds.

On the way back to Leeds, the taxi driver realised that they were being followed by one of the bouncers who was stood outside the club earlier. This was very alarming because Connor was convinced that his girlfriend had been deliberately spiked in the club. Also, since he had been shouting at the bouncers, telling them that his girl had been spiked and that he was going to call the police, this might have made the bouncers paranoid.

Connor believed that the guy behind the bar must have spiked his girlfriend's drink, and that he was deliberately thrown out of the club and separated from his girlfriend. He pondered that it was an organised group, including the bartenders and bouncers, who wanted to take advantage of his girlfriend. Otherwise they had no reason to follow their taxi, unless they thought that he was going to report this incident to the police and wanted to know where he lived in case of any later repercussions.

Something was fishy, either way.

He asked the driver to come off in Mirfield and drive into the new housing estate to try and lose the car that was following them. However, the bouncer was relentless, and he followed as they came off the motorway which only further confirmed what he was doing.

The taxi managed to lose the bouncer at a set of traffic lights, driving into a large estate where the couple got out and hid in a supermarket. After waiting a little while, they arranged another taxi which happened to be me as I was on my way back from Huddersfield. I couldn't believe what I was hearing; it was surreal. The story sounded like a Hollywood blockbuster.

As he recounted the situation, Connor was convinced that the club had a secret organisation of spiking drinks. Since Huddersfield isn't a big town, they probably realised that the couple were not local and decided to take their chances. Unfortunately for him, he couldn't prove his theory.

I advised him to speak to the police who could check the CCTV cameras in the club in case they witness the culprit who spiked her drink, but Connor insisted that he would pay a visit to the club with his friends because he wanted to confront them himself.

This sounded a bit too crazy to me, but this guy was rightfully angry, given the state of his girlfriend. I also suggested that he take her to the hospital and make sure she's alright, but he didn't think that was necessary and just wanted to get her home.

I dropped the couple in Leeds, wishing I could find out

whether he went back to the club with his mates and what happened. His girlfriend was lucky to have him there, otherwise the situation could have been different if she was alone.

If the staff at the club have organised a tactic to spike the drinks they serve to females, they must target vulnerable girls and young students in Huddersfield. Although there is no way to know if the drink coming straight from the bar has been spiked, people need to be extra vigilant that such things can happen.

He's not drunk

One night, I saw a group of people surrounding someone who was lying on the ground. Full of dread, I worried that it could be my customers since the pickup point was nearby. One of them noticed me in the car and ran over frantically, waving his arms in the air. I locked my car doors immediately, as there was no chance that I would take a completely drunk person home.

My car window was down two inches, leaving enough gap for the young man to ask me if I could move the car closer to his friend. I moved my head from left to right, indicating a firm refusal, and told him to allow his friend to recover for about twenty minutes to the point that he can at least get up and walk around, and then arrange another taxi.

The boy said that his friend wasn't drunk and to not worry about him vomiting in the car. Rather, he had just taken a drug called ketamine which numbs the body, hence why his friend had lost function in his legs. Ketamine, which is used as a horse tranquiliser, has recently become a very popular drug on the student clubbing scene.

I was interested as this was my first encounter with someone high on ketamine. After hearing a lot about this drug from other student customers, I went over to have a look at the collapsed boy. I noticed the effects of this drug as the boy was just really drowsy and smiling away in his own little planet, talking to his friends like a five-year old trapped in an adult's body.

I agreed to take him home and helped him into the car, whilst advising his friends how dangerous it is to take drugs that are not fit for human consumption. This young man had become immobile, with no feeling in his legs, so out of it that he was smiling whilst playing with his girlfriend's hair throughout the journey.

I was really surprised that everyone else was having a laugh amongst themselves, ignoring their friend's condition. I personally felt it was very dangerous for someone to be in this state, since if he was on his own then anything could happen to him as he was totally helpless. During the journey, there were no signs of vomit, but if I was him, I would rather vomit and sober up than be stuck in his helpless state.

Apparently, it has similar effects to cocaine, snorted in the same powder form and used to induce sedation and numbness. This is what makes ketamine attractive, as it is three times cheaper than cocaine but apparently is considered just as cool. Since then, I have picked up passengers after a night out who have taken this drug and then suffered from heavy nose bleeds, looking like they've been in a nasty fight.

I cannot imagine the long-term damage that ketamine has

on the brain. Parents would be petrified if they knew about some of the substances that students take whilst at university. Unfortunately, if someone gets involved with the wrong crowd then rest assured, they will be trying all sorts of dangerous drugs.

Suicide

First year students can sometimes struggle to have a social life at university, especially if they don't have many contact hours, and instead spend a lot of their time isolated from others. A grieving passenger told me that her friend had hung himself in his bedroom because he was struggling to get along with the people in his accommodation block. Sadly, the young man couldn't cope with the loneliness and became depressed, which resulted in him committing suicide.

Developing social skills to go out, make new friends or even just to get along with people is very important, but this ability is now deteriorating. The constant use of social media and smart phones has had a damaging effect on this basic human skill for the younger generations. Unfortunately, people are too caught up in themselves to develop successful relationships with others.

The statistics for the number of students suffering from anxiety and depression in the U.K. is astronomical and heart-breaking. Lack of human connection and empathy will always result in anarchy, leading to suicidal tendencies and often, regrettably, suicide. This young man could have lived a great life, if only there was more understanding and awareness.

Once, a cabbie was taking a drunken girl home from town centre. When he arrived at her destination, he waited for her to get out of the car and when she didn't, he turned around to see if she had fallen asleep. That's when he saw she was covered in blood, sitting in a pool of it in the back. Mortified, he jumped out of the car and called for an ambulance and the police, telling the authorities that she had attempted to commit suicide in the back of his taxi.

When the emergency services arrived, it was determined that during the journey, the drunken girl had taken out her makeup mirror and somehow accidentally cut her hand open. In her drunken state and with a cut that deep, she had not realised that she was bleeding profusely from her right palm.

The vehicle was stained in so much blood that the driver had to go through insurance in order to remove the fabric seats and suede door panels. It looked like a murder scene.

Parental Supervision

A young student got into my taxi and asked if I could get her some cocaine. I asked her why she would want to waste her money and risk her health on snorting crap like that, when she couldn't guarantee what would be mixed into these diluted substances.

To my surprise, she told me that her father had taken many different types of drugs over the years, and that sometimes when she's at home she would take drugs with her parents. My naivety was apparent as I had always believed that no parent would normalise drugs to their child. Surely it's a bad habit, and we wouldn't want our children making the same mistakes as we may have.

I knew, however, that I had no chance of convincing her to stop snorting cocaine, especially if her parents were relaxed about drug use. I suppose, on a positive note, it is better to take drugs under parental supervision as opposed to someone else giving you something that could be a lot more dangerous and life-threatening, such as heroin. PG rated drugs are better, I guess.

The Cabbie's Son

Summer is like an endless series of Friday nights in student-infested areas. The city of Leeds houses almost two hundred thousand students in total, so it becomes difficult to see the green grass in Hyde Park during the summer when it is covered with beer bottles. Not all students behave this way, but it's a shame that some are so disrespectful to their host city.

The smoke from cannabis and barbeques coats the air, especially during the Leeds carnival when these scents replace the surrounding oxygen. Whilst there are police patrolling the park, you'll notice that they naively pretend they can't smell any drugs. I suppose realistically, they can't arrest everyone in a public park for smoking cannabis. I don't think there is a police station in the country that can contain thousands of stoned students.

One group of college students got into a taxi after getting together to smoke weed in the park. The driver couldn't ignore the strong smell of marijuana and began to advise the boys about the dangerous effects of smoking on their health. During the conversation, the driver told them that his son attends the same college, prompting the students to ask for his son's name. To their surprise, the driver's son turned out to be one of their mates: one that was also a regular member of their smoking sessions.

The students, feeling high and silly, began chuckling in the back of the taxi. Although they were the ones that had smoked weed, the driver was the one who got paranoid. He repeatedly asked them if they knew his son and why they were laughing. Eventually, they told the driver that they knew him but redacted how good he was at rolling up joints. The students thought it was hilarious and still joke about it at college when they're smoking with the cabbie's son.

Powder My Nose

picked up a young, well-dressed couple on a busy weekend to take them home after a long night out. Stuart sat in the front next to me, whilst his girlfriend sheepishly climbed into the back. They were both in their early twenties and had graduated a few years ago, now working and living together.

I alerted Stuart about the suspicious patch of white dust on his nose. Instead of self-consciously wiping it off, he seemed to be pleased that I had noticed it. I think he wanted to leave it there as some sort of proof that he was cool.

Innocently, I complimented his shirt without knowing that he would take it as an invitation to boast. He went off on one, bragging about how many Armani shirts he had in his wardrobe. His girlfriend tried to contribute to the conversation, but he wasn't having any of it and dismissed her. Clearly, he loved talking about himself and hearing only his own voice. I couldn't stop laughing at his immature behaviour.

On route to their house, his girlfriend alerted us to the fact that she was feeling peckish and wanted to stop at McDonalds for some food. When we went into the drive-thru, Stuart was very rude to the girls taking their order. Impatiently, he told them to hurry up as it's a fast-food joint and so he wanted his food fast. Mr. Big-head was calling all the shots that night.

Whilst we waited in the car park for their food to arrive, Stuart went inside to powder his nose – I assumed he meant this as euphemism for using the loo, although I couldn't be sure with him. A few minutes later, the food arrived and then we waited for Stuart to get back from the toilets. After a good ten to fifteen minutes talking to his girlfriend, I decided to go inside and see where he was. I was planning to remind him that it was a fast-food joint so he should hurry up.

Upon entering the restaurant, I found him straight away. There he was, emptying his pockets onto the table whilst some police officers searched him for drugs. From what I understood, the police officers were in the McDonalds grabbing a coffee when they noticed cool Stuart's white dust on his nose. Suspicious of his appearance, they decided to search him and found a small bag of cocaine in his possession.

I knew this idiot would have a long night ahead of him at the police station, so I went back to the car and told his girlfriend about what had happened. We agreed to drop her off home. As for Stuart, he might want to wipe that dust from his nose next time. It's definitely not cool getting arrested in McDonalds.

The Student Stripper

It was in the middle of the week, approximately two o'clock in the morning, when I received an alert for a pickup outside of a strip joint in Leeds. She was a young lady and looked quite exhausted, probably due to only just finishing her shift at the club. Claire was working as a stripper to pay for her education and living expenses whilst studying medicine at the University of Leeds.

On her first night, she earned one hundred and fifty pounds from an old Australian businessman who happened to fall for her beauty and charm. She had been working as a stripper for the past two years and managed to save enough money to afford a deposit to purchase a house in Leeds.

I asked her how her fellow students felt about her working as a stripper, but she said that no one knows what she does except for her parents, in order to avoid any unnecessary gossip and drama at university. She worked in a closed environment where the customers were not allowed to touch any of the girls in order to keep them safe from harassment.

Nevertheless, she had been groped many times by customers who were too drunk; luckily those customers would be promptly thrown out of the joint. She also made a fair point: this behaviour isn't any different from what women encounter from men in a nightclub, or even on public transport nowadays. She acknowledged that she would never do this job if she was financially stable or if it wasn't so expensive to be a student.

To meet someone in her position training to be a doctor in the future was an eye-opener. She took this unconventional job so she could train for a professional role that is both respectable and crucial to society. Although I felt that there were other jobs she could do without perverse males attempting to touch her, the money was very attractive and ultimately it was her choice.

I believe it will take her many years as a doctor before she exceeds her salary as a stripper, twisted as that may be.

Weekly Casino Budget

I always enjoy picking up people after they've been to the casino because it's interesting to find out if they've made any big winnings, or even more entertaining, any losses. On this occasion, an Arab student from Bahrain got into the car and, when I asked him if he had won anything, he replied with a huge cheesy grin on his face and told me he has just lost his weekly casino budget again. Apparently, he has a limit of three hundred pounds a week.

I couldn't believe that this guy had a weekly casino budget which equated to twelve hundred pounds per month. Jokingly, I told him that I couldn't even afford to save the amount he blows every month, and that he'd be better off transferring it directly into my account instead.

Saeed was from a very affluent family that owns businesses in the Middle East. From his smile, I would assume he had had a big win, but really he didn't feel like he had lost anything at the casino. Even if he had won a few thousand pounds, it wouldn't make any difference to his lifestyle. It was just a bit of fun and part of being a rich student in the UK; there was a genuine lack of appreciation.

One night, I picked up four teenage boys from the casino. I had never seen a group of grown lads so ecstatic in my life. I didn't have to ask the guys if they had won anything because I knew from their victorious walk out of the front doors. Mike had only won thirty-five pounds, but their excitement would suggest they had won about five hundred pounds.

The main man, Mike, sat in the front passenger seat with the winnings and was on the phone sharing the news with his dad. The boys headed to McDonalds to celebrate their victory with a Big Mac. They insisted that I join them at McDonalds, so I happily obliged and ordered a coffee. Normally I don't accept food from passengers when I take them to a fast food joint, but this was an exception as it made me feel good to take part in their joy.

Their gratitude and happiness for their humble winnings was a real pleasure to see in a young group of guys.

Rich Student

One night I picked up a couple who were out celebrating as Michael had finally received his compensation money from a taxi vehicle accident in which he was sat in the back. He had won eleven thousand pounds because a police vehicle had driven into the back of his taxi one day whilst he was on his way home from work.

At the moment of impact, Michael looked back to see what had happened and realised it was a female driver in a police vehicle who was holding a mobile phone to her ear. He noticed she was still on the phone even after the collision, so Michael alerted the driver and they both got out to look at the damage at the back of the vehicle. The lady police officer got out and profusely apologised, acknowledging her fault.

The taxi driver complained that it wouldn't have happened if she wasn't on her phone, but she completely denied this fact. That was until the driver warned her about the collision being recorded on the CCTV cameras in his cab, along with Michael as a witness to corroborate that she was on her phone.

Michael claimed compensation for whiplash to his spine, as well as the stress and anxiety he suffered from fear of giving evidence against the police, in case of any consequences. Apparently, Michael was scared to leave his apartment for a few months after the incident. To help him overcome the trauma suffered from his accident, his doctor prescribed him some medication for depression and he was also referred for counselling at the university.

Whilst he was telling me his story, the couple had a big and proud smile on their faces and his girlfriend was chuckling the whole time. They were both obviously pleased with the large pay-out, looking forward to their upcoming trip to Thailand in the summer.

I guess in a strange way, he had been lucky.

The Compensation Culture

I collected a young male in his thirties from the General Infirmary at midday. He had a bandage wrapped around his right hand and wrist and looked very frustrated. When I greeted him, his response was minimal which indicated that he didn't want to converse, perhaps mainly because he didn't want to explain his injury.

During the journey, I was driving down a slip road that merged onto a dual carriageway when I used the brakes just before joining. This gently threw the passenger forward. Suddenly, the man was shouting and screaming about his hand, complaining that I should have not used the car brakes so harshly.

I admitted to the customer that I did break promptly, but it couldn't have affected his bandaged hand in the slightest. It was obvious that he was exaggerating, and being familiar with such people, I could predict where this was all going. He was trying to make some easy money through a potential compensation claim.

He moaned that he may have to go back to the hospital for another X-ray as he may have fractured his hand now. Tired of his indirect threats, I told him that nothing had happened and to stop exaggerating. I said that he already had the bandage on his hand, but if he wanted to go back to the hospital then I would happily turn around and deliver him.

This temporarily silenced him, and he didn't tell me to head back to the hospital, which made me sure about his whole act. Then, I noticed him take out his mobile phone, and I assumed he was recording for evidence this time. He began the confrontation again.

"So why were you driving so fast?"

Now convinced that he was recording the conversation, I responded with deliberate ignorance as if I didn't know what he was talking about.

"Driving fast where? What do you mean?"

By not complying with his plan, I had aggravated him. He warned that he was going to report the incident to the council and took a photo of my taxi license badge.

Patronisingly, I told him he was more than welcome to complain about the journey and wished him all the best. He was quiet for the rest of the trip when he realised his act wouldn't work this time. He'd given up and placed his phone back into his pocket.

I was still unsatisfied with his drama and thought that he should be taught a lesson for making my job more difficult. So, as I pulled up outside his house, I deliberately slammed the breaks hard. This wound him up again and he started shouting and threatening that he was going to report me.

He got out of the car and made a recording of my car and

number plate. I totally ignored him and drove off, never to hear anything from him ever again.

If you're going to make an issue out of nothing, then I will at least give you an issue first!

Charitable Taxi Driver

Freddie told me about his encounter with a taxi driver when he was a student in London many years ago. Despite there being some truth to taxi drivers in London being rude, this driver was actually a chatty bloke who truly enjoyed his job in the capital city.

Whilst working in the taxi trade, he had managed to raise five children, all of which were university graduates that had since married and settled into their own lives. He was excited about his own life, since for his thirtieth marriage anniversary his wife and he were going to celebrate with a trip to New York.

During their journey, the driver began to tell Freddie about the experience he's gained during his twenty-five years as a taxi driver, meeting people from all over the world. In fact, not only has he been meeting people, but he boasted about how he'd managed to get in bed with both male and female customers. He continued, humbly describing himself as charitable by offering people the option to pay for the journey through sexual favours instead of money.

This alarmed Freddie as to where this conversation was going and so he jumped out of the car at the next set of traffic lights. He ran as fast as he could through the local park for fifteen minutes, not looking back until he felt completely rid of the driver – and rid of the distasteful suggestion too.

I wonder how the cabbie was able to afford a trip to New York with his wife when his method of payment hasn't exactly been monetary...

Georgia on My Mind

Ironically, Georgia dressed up as a nun for the local pub crawl. As we travelled to Headingley, she told me about a taxi encounter she'd had when she was in Birmingham. The driver was singing 'Georgia On My Mind' by Willie Nelson.

At first, she thought it was innocent and funny, but he continued to sing the song whilst playing it on the sound system throughout the journey. He told her that ever since the song was released, he'd sing it for his passengers with the name Georgia. Not only that, the nutcase also had a fetish that he only dated women called Georgia.

Georgia, now a bit freaked out at his sleazy suggestion, remained on edge for the rest of the trip. Obviously there was no way she would hang out with this creep. When they arrived at her destination, he asked her if she would go on a date with him. She flatly refused, telling him she wasn't interested and that the twenty-plus year gap between them meant he was old enough to be her father.

Cheekily, he persisted by asking for a peck on the cheek before she left. Georgia again refused and stated very clearly that she didn't want to kiss him. As she nervously got out of the car, he quickly slapped her on the bum. In her humiliation, she told him to get lost and ran off. She called the taxi firm and told them about what had happened, but she never got any feedback and wasn't sure if there was an outcome.

Perhaps he is still harassing Georgia's to this day.

Touchy Taxi Driver

On a warm summer's evening, Harry caught a taxi home after spending the day at his friend's barbeque party. He decided to leave at half past ten, as he wanted to get up early the next morning for his nephew's christening.

In his shorts, Harry got into the front passenger seat next to the driver. The driver turned out to be very friendly from the moment he picked Harry up. Five minutes into the conversation, he slapped Harry's leg whilst laughing about something. Harry was only wearing shorts and so he felt a bit uneasy with this action. Internally, Harry excused the driver as perhaps a touchy guy that simply didn't realise that he was wearing shorts, so he let it go.

A few minutes later the driver did the same again, but this time he kept his hand on Harry's leg and gently squeezed it for a couple of seconds. This was beyond excusable now, and Harry felt that the driver was most definitely trying something with him.

Harry felt extremely uncomfortable and wanted to address it but couldn't find the opportunity to do so as the driver was relentless in his conversation, not giving a moment's pause. Instead, Harry moved his legs away from the driver to the left side, placing his hand to cover his right leg in case the driver tried to touch him again.

After a painfully long amount of time, they finally arrived at his house. Assuming he was now safe, Harry rushed out of the car, but not before the driver tried to pull his shorts down. Shocked at this attempt, Harry quickly grabbed onto them and managed to save himself from being exposed. He pulled away from the vehicle and began shouting at the driver.

"What the hell are you doing?"

The driver apologised and promised that his intention wasn't to pull Harry's pants down. He claimed that he was trying to call him back to check the car seats and ensure that he'd taken all of his belongings before he left.

At the time Harry was convinced that the driver had made a genuine mistake, perhaps out of wishful thinking. Reflecting back at the whole encounter however, he regretted that he never reported the driver. He realised that this man in his mid-fifties was very sly and experienced in his perverted ways, smooth talking his way out of accountability.

Needless to say, Harry didn't use that taxi firm again, nor does he ever sit in the front seat of a cab – with or without his shorts.

The Numbers Game

One night, I collected a group of student girls on their way to town for a night out. Since they were a little tipsy, the girls were chatting away to me. They asked me about the weirdest experience I have had during my time as a taxi driver. So, I entertained them through my encounter with one particularly strange passenger.

Miles got into the back of my car and began the usual chatter as he asked me how my night was going. He then told me he had just left his one-night stand, emphasising that it was quite awkward. Hesitantly, I asked why it was awkward.

"The other guy was too short, but we managed to get things sorted anyway."

Since I didn't respond, he continued.

"I told him I was really good at it, but he wouldn't believe me."

Miles proclaimed this several times, trying to prompt me to ask him exactly what his talent was. My curiosity took over and I decided to give in as he was dying to share it with me.

Obviously, his answer was oral sex. I didn't react or respond to this and continued driving the car. I felt that he was expecting me to say something, but I remained quiet to stop the conversation from developing any further. On arrival before he left the car, he asked me if I was interested.

I looked at him calmly. "Don't waste my time. Goodbye Miles."

A few weeks later, I picked up the same guy but from a different location in Leeds. I recognised him immediately, as I often do with passengers that I've had conversations with; but I could not forget this guy.

Miles got into the back of the cab and asked me how my night had been so far again. He proceeded to tell me that he had just come out from a one-night stand and was headed home. Here we go again, I thought.

I asked him how his night had been, and he said that it was very awkward. I was about to ask if it was awkward because the other guy was too short, but that would alert him about our previous conversation and perhaps he would become reserved. So, I decided to let him continue and see where he was going with his story this time.

Miles repeated that the other guy was too short, but they eventually managed. He also said that the other guy wouldn't believe that he was really good at 'it.'

I realised that this guy had refined a chat-up line for taxi drivers. He was obviously playing a numbers game which probably worked for him sometimes, otherwise he wouldn't be so persistent.

The girls enjoyed the story and were laughing throughout the journey. After dropping them off in town, I received a job alert to collect someone else a short distance away. To my surprise, it was Miles for the third time! I wanted to go back and tell the girls; I had never been so spooked in my life.

After hearing his chat-up line yet again, I later decided that I would have to tell him next time that his genius chat-up line is being wasted on me.

He's in a Hurry

When Merlina was living in the Netherlands, she'd often catch a cab home after a night out. In the Netherlands, taxis usually have a card payment system affixed in the vehicle. One time when she had arrived at her destination, she realised that the taxi driver didn't have this system and unfortunately, she didn't have any cash to use instead.

The taxi driver refused to take her to an ATM machine, telling her he was in a hurry to get to his next customer. Shamelessly, however, he suggested two options: she could either have sex with him or hand over her mobile phone until she paid him. Obviously she wasn't going to have sex with this insolent man, nor did she want to give her mobile phone as she didn't think she'd get it back.

Merlina was absolutely petrified and puzzled, crying as she was unsure what to do with this pervert who had no time to take her to an ATM machine, but enough time for sex. She finally succumbed to giving her mobile phone. Although this was a risky decision, she managed to get her phone back after paying him the next day. She never reported the driver.

Gutters and Gutted

One afternoon, I received a job alert to collect a passenger from an industrial estate outside of Leeds. Unusually, and sounding very upset and anxious, the customer called me and asked how long I was going to be. I sensed this guy was in a desperate hurry.

When I arrived, Paul was already on the phone to someone else and jumped straight into the back of my car. He told me to put my foot down all the way to Harrogate, approximately fourteen miles away. During the journey, from what I understood, he was telling his partner not to worry and to stay calm. He reassured her that he would be there in half an hour and that everything would be fine once he was with her.

Then he made another call, although this one was more aggressive. He told the person on the other end to stop what they're doing and leave the house immediately. Using every swear word that he could think of, Paul threatened that he was going to break someone's legs.

I had never seen someone so furious. It was the first time that I felt scared, even though the passenger had no problem with me. His rage made him capable of doing allot of harm without realising. He was a muscular man and emanated strong energy. Finally, I received an explanation for our mission.

Paul had arranged for a drainage company to replace gutters on the roof of his house. His partner had taken a day off from work in order to be at home for when the workers came. Whilst the guys were on site, one of the workers asked Paul's girlfriend if he could use the toilet. She happily obliged, allowing him to enter the property.

After a while, she went upstairs to make sure that everything was alright, only to find the worker standing in the bathroom and holding her underwear in his hands. She had hung her washed underwear on the central heating radiators to dry. Upon seeing this sight, she froze. She ran straight into her bedroom and locked the door. Petrified, she called her partner telling him what had happened whilst crying uncontrollably. She was too petrified to leave the bedroom.

I barely stopped the car before he jumped out and rushed into his house. I bolted off myself, as I didn't want to be a witness. I hoped that the worker had enough sense to leave the site, otherwise he was about to be a dead man for sure.

Snapchat Cabbie

Tracey and her friends were on their way to party in town, when the driver asked them to record a Snapchat video in his cab. The driver turned up the music up and told the girls to start dancing. Originally, they thought that he was asking Tracey to record it on her Snapchat, since they were the ones going clubbing.

But no, to their surprise, the cabbie wanted the video on his Snapchat story. He recorded the girls dancing in the background, to look as though he's having fun with his girlfriends in the car.

The girls couldn't stop laughing at what he had just done. They recorded the video from his phone and added it to their own Snapchat story, telling all of their student friends about eccentric taxi driver.

Stalking Taxi Driver

Originally from Norwich, Stacey was studying in Leeds when she told me about the time she headed to her friend's house for pre-drinks, or prinks as she would say. The driver, Tony, informed her that it was his first shift as a cab driver and that Stacey was special as she was the first customer he had picked up. Although he managed to get lost, taking fifteen minutes for a five-minute journey, she didn't complain since it was his first day at work.

He asked Stacey where she would be going after pre-drinks and she mentioned some of the different bars they intended to go to after a few hours at her friend's place. As they arrived at her friend's house, the driver said he might pop into town and join her for a drink if he spots her in one of the bars. Stacey kindly welcomed him, assuming it was probably a joke and expecting nothing from it.

Of course, the driver turned out to be an oddity and later that evening when she was out in the city with her friends, he came over and reintroduced himself to a confounded Stacey.

"Hi Stacey, I'm the taxi driver. I picked you up earlier."

Mr. Taxi Driver paid for the round of drinks the girls had ordered at the bar and then joined Stacey and her friends at their table. The girls were friendly, surprised at the bizarre situation of being stuck with this strange cabbie on their table. He tried to engage in their conversations, but instead kept interrupting with his unwanted opinions. He was trying very hard to be the centre of attention.

The girls didn't know what to do and were growing uncomfortable. They anxiously wanted to get rid of this guy interfering with their girly night. They finished their drinks and hurriedly left to the next bar, hoping he wouldn't follow them all night.

But Mr. Taxi Driver was determined; he followed them to the next bar as though it wasn't obvious enough that they were escaping him.

"Hi girls, what drinks are you having?"

Not wanting to be in his debt again, the girls refused to let him buy their drinks as he'd already paid for the first round. But he insisted, paid for the second round and once again, followed them to their table. The girls were frustrated, wondering how this weirdo had suddenly become a part of their lives.

During their awkward conversation, Mr. Taxi Driver excused himself to use the toilet, which gave the girls an opportunity to break free. They desperately darted out of the bar, got into a city taxi and made their way to the opposite side of town to some other bars. They successfully avoided Mr. Taxi Driver for the rest of the night.

I asked her why she didn't tell the police or report this to the Leeds City Council. They felt that he didn't really do anything wrong, apart from paying for their drinks twice. He may have been a loner just looking for some company. Looking back at the whole encounter, Stacey seemed to find it hilarious. On the upside, at least, they didn't have to pay for two rounds of drinks at the start of their night.

The Self-Employed Physiotherapist

Dressed in a skirt and heels, Shanice arranged a taxi to town on a summer evening to meet some friends for a birthday party. She was a self-employed physiotherapist and whilst she was in the cab, she received a call from a customer who enquired about her hourly rates for a physiotherapy session.

After she finished her conversation with a potential client, the cab driver became inquisitive, asking Shanice how much she would charge for thirty minutes. She told him that she charges seventy-five pounds per hour. He turned around with a surprised look.

"Everyone else charges for half an hour. What are you going to do to me that will make me go for longer?"

She quickly realised that there was a misunderstanding, as the taxi driver was talking as though she was an escort. Now embarrassed at the driver's confusion and insinuation, she explained herself.

"I work as a physiotherapist and charge by the hour. I'm not an escort!"

Tickled at this change of events, the driver laughed and apologised for his misunderstanding. An uncomfortable silence filled the car and she couldn't imagine what this fifty-year old man was thinking as he watched her talk on the phone from the rear-view mirror. For the rest of the journey, he drove with a sleazy grin on his face, and she swiftly left the car on arrival.

Jehovah's Witness

Samantha caught a cab late at night whilst she was very drunk. Ironically, the driver was a Jehovah's Witness. The conversation progressed, and he began talking about how important his belief was to him.

Samantha told him that she was a Christian, but this guy was determined that he could convert her to his beliefs as she already believed in Jesus. He was babbling all the way to her apartment and decided to log off the system so he could continue to talk to her. He was parked outside her flat for over ten minutes.

By this point, Samantha was dozing off in the back of the cab and just wanted to get to bed. She didn't want to be rude whilst he was talking to her, so she gave him her mobile number. She promised the driver that they would discuss this subject on another day when she was sober.

The following week, Samantha was bombarded with text messages from the cabbie, full of passages from the gospel.

Eventually she had to block his number after her boyfriend clocked on that she was being harassed.

You never know, he could still turn up at her door.

Lazy People

Times have changed dramatically since I was an eighteen-year-old student. Back in 1995, we used to walk everywhere we went and never considered the option of a taxi. If someone had told me then that there would be students booking an online taxi for a third of a mile in the middle of summer and paying three pounds, then I think we would genuinely believe those students were mentally disturbed. Now it's a completely different world: a world where I have picked up passengers only to drop them off at the bottom of the street. Literally.

Once, I collected three boys to travel no more than two blocks away on a pleasantly warm summer's day. It took me five minutes to get to their pickup point, in which I'm sure they could have reached their destination if they had walked. I wasn't bothered as I was making money and could happily do fifty short trips daily, but at the same time I couldn't help but ask why they needed to get a taxi for this.

In response, this young man just looked at me and shrugged

his shoulders. That was probably the best answer I would get. It was obvious that these guys were bone idle as they couldn't be arsed walking down the street. The shoulder shrug basically meant 'Why not?' – which I guess is the popular rationale nowadays.

I suppose it is also partly due to the convenience that internet-based taxi firms bring to the market, making it too easy for a taxi to arrive in front of you within as little as a minute's notice. This has been a game-changer, since you don't even need to call the taxi office for an ETA. The phone app allows you to see exactly where the driver is, usually only a couple of minutes away, and you can contact them directly.

But there are only two challenges with using an internet-based taxi service. First, you have to ensure that your phone has enough charge at the end of the night so that you can order a cab. Second, you can't be too drunk that you input the wrong destination and end up two hundred miles away from where you actually want to be.

I had a customer who wanted to travel to a street which was only a mile away, but she accidentally added another street with the same name that was three hours and one hundred and eighty miles away. You see, taxi drivers don't always confirm the details of a journey as they assume that the customer has chosen the right location. Luckily in this case she was sober, so we quickly realised we were going in the wrong direction. However, had she been intoxicated and fallen asleep in the back of the cab, it would have been a field day for me but a real nightmare for the customer who would have to pay hundreds of pounds to be stuck on the other side of the country.

Wrong Destination

One taxi driver picked up a very drunk passenger from Leeds city centre, not realising he had selected his home location in Birmingham instead of his student accommodation in Headingley that was only two miles away. The passenger was so drunk that he fell asleep as soon as he got into the car.

On arrival to Birmingham, the driver woke up the passenger who was in complete shock to be outside his parent's house. He was one hundred and thirty miles away from where he needed to be and incurred a loss of two hundred and forty pounds.

This poor kid, now wide awake, was in tears realising his costly mistake. He definitely didn't want to go inside and confront his parents about what had happened. The driver acknowledged the young student's dilemma and since he would be driving back to Leeds anyway, he offered to take him for free. This was a profitable day for the driver, raking in a decent wage for a journey that would have only been a few pounds and a good deed for the stumped kid.

Pepper Spray

Sometimes taxi businesses that accept cash payments face dodgy customers who have no intention of paying, and instead plan to do a runner when near to their destination. Due to such incidents, drivers can become excessively vigilant and paranoid about not receiving a payment.

Passenger Tony told me about an encounter with a cabbie ten years ago, when he caught a taxi from Bolton to Bury with his friends for a night out. As soon as the trio sat in the back of the cab, the driver demanded twenty pounds in advance. The guys thought it was unfair to pay upfront, so they refused to do so until the journey was completed. The driver, now even more concerned about not receiving his payment, was getting very agitated and was demanding the money, but the guys remained firm with their decision to pay on arrival.

Then, the driver pulled over to the side of the road and pulled out his pepper spray, squirting all three boys in the face. Temporarily blind and shocked, the boys yelled as they jumped out of the taxi to escape the driver's insanity.

Tony and his friends were in no condition to retaliate after what just happened. They reported the incident to the police who came to the scene and escorted the guys to a local hospital for emergency treatment. Apparently, the driver was arrested and charged appropriately. His licence was confiscated by the local authorities, making sure this doesn't happen again.

Reflecting on the encounter, Tony thought that if one of them had sat next to the driver, he wouldn't have been so paranoid about the payment. But because all three got into the back, he thought the guys were planning to quickly jump out and run off once they arrived.

Driving an online-based taxi guarantees payment, as all funds are automatically deducted from the passenger's account. There is no worry about anyone refusing to pay or running off before doing so. In fact, I have rarely spoken to a customer about the fare since they have already settled it when booking the journey on the phone app; we talk about everything else besides the fare. Sometimes though, the customers forget about the payment method and begin pulling out their wallets at the end of a journey, getting me all excited for a nice tip – until they realise.

On one occasion, a young man was travelling to a small village called Wetherby which is approximately ten miles outside Leeds. He decided to get out of the car and run off as the driver approached Wetherby's town centre, not realising that he had already paid automatically from his account. He must have felt like a real fool when he later noticed this transaction on his account – he certainly looked like a fool to the driver!

Taxi drivers that handle cash can be very vulnerable targets when they are carrying a full night's worth of wages. Anything is possible; you could be set up by being drawn to a location where there are people waiting to rob you at the end of a busy night. Situations where people have refused to pay have resulted in violence, and taxi drivers have been involved in fights where they have been brutally attacked or even, unfortunately, killed.

But alas, sometimes this leads to excessive paranoia, and doesn't end well for innocent people like Tony and his friends.

My Longest Journey

One of my longer journeys was to Manchester Airport with a man that I picked up from a hotel in Leeds. Frank had originally set the destination for the train station around the corner, but then he suddenly changed the route directly to Manchester Airport. Frank's flight was for a work-related meeting in Brussels, as part of his job as a brewer.

Why was he late if the meeting was so important? Well, it turned out that he had another more urgent meeting. He had sacrificed some of his time for a lady on Sweet Street, next to his hotel. This street is one of the few streets in England where prostitution is legalised. In other words, the police turn a blind eye. Frank treated himself to a hooker, delaying his trip to the airport.

So, I drove sixty-five miles on the motorway, at a surge price of 1.3x which easily paid me a hundred pounds. However, this happiness was short-lived because after a few days I received a letter from the Manchester Metropolitan Police for a speeding ticket. According to the speed cameras, I was driving 64 miles per hour in a 60 mile per hour zone. This earned me a whopping hundred pound fine and three lucky points on my licence, running the journey into a loss. This was my longest, most expensive and most consequential journey yet.

Admittedly, I sped up for the passenger. Whilst Frank relieved his pressure, the pressure was put on silly old me to make sure he arrived on time. After receiving this fine for speeding, I never went out of my way to exceed any speeding limits for customers. It is their responsibility to get a taxi on time, and life is not a Hollywood movie where taxi drivers are there to serve their customers' crazy missions.

Budapest Rats

Sarah and her friends were in Budapest when they decided to move to a different hostel because of the horrendously shabby condition of theirs. They had terrifying rats running wild and one of the girls was even woken up as a large rodent scurried along her bed. She screamed as though her life depended on it, which it probably did. The girls didn't sleep for the rest of the night and made sure they were out of the place first thing in the morning.

The next morning, the girls found another hostel nearby. They had arranged for a taxi to drop them off because of their luggage, the heat and not knowing their exact whereabouts. The taxi driver took them on a thirty-five-minute detour around Budapest. When they finally arrived, they were shocked to realise that it was in the same location as their previous hostel, just further down the road. The girls were furious when the driver demanded forty Euros. It was obvious that he had taken them for a long ride hoping they wouldn't suspect that it was just down the road, especially since he entered the road from the opposite end.

The driver pretended to not understand why they were angry, nor why they were refusing to pay him. He relentlessly demanded the money. The headstrong girls sat in the car and remained quiet. Eventually, the con merchant realised that they were not falling for his cheeky detour. He finally agreed to a payment of five Euros, which is all it cost the girls to receive a great tour of Budapest.

The Thief

After a long night of drinking, Gary and his girlfriend got a taxi home from the city centre, which would usually cost them no more than fifteen pounds. On arrival, the driver asked for twenty-five pounds. This infuriated Gary as he refused to pay the extortionate fare. The driver was stubborn, demanding the payment whist claiming that busy weekend nights means higher taxi charges.

Gary didn't want to spend the night arguing with the driver as he wanted to get his drunk girlfriend home, so he agreed to pay the money and gave the driver a fifty-pound note. Whilst Gary was getting his girlfriend out of the car, the driver scrunched up the change and handed it to Gary. Assuming he was given twenty-five pounds in change, Gary didn't bother checking and was too busy trying to stop his girlfriend from falling over.

The next morning, he retrieved the change from his pocket to find only fifteen pounds, meaning he had actually paid thirty-five pounds for a fifteen-pound journey.

Two weeks later, the couple were buying a gift for a friend's birthday when they caught a taxi from the shopping mall to get to the party. To Gary's surprise, their driver was the same one that had ripped them off before, so he alerted his girlfriend. This time, the journey was definitely not more than twenty pounds, but they decided to take a scenic detour since they wanted to pick up a bottle of wine too.

When they finally arrived, they quickly got out and started walking towards the venue of the birthday party. The driver jumped out to tell the couple that they forgot to pay him. Gary turned around and reminded the driver of the twenty pounds advance that he had helped himself to previously and that he could keep the change too. The driver began shouting and swearing, as he threatened to call the police.

The couple ignored him and carried on walking, whilst the driver mumbled in his own foreign lingo, experiencing the reality of not being paid this time. It was a really satisfying moment of justice for Gary and his girlfriend.

Another one of my passengers reminisced about his eighteenth birthday. He was so drunk that he didn't have the ability to go and withdraw money from the cash machine to pay for the taxi. Innocently, he gave his debit card to the driver and told him the pin number to withdraw the money for him. The next day, the boy realised that the cabbie had helped himself to a hundred pounds instead of just ten. Happy birthday!

Overcharged

One night I collected a male from the KFC in York, not realising he was extremely drunk. Sean wanted to eat his fried chicken as soon as he sat in the car and wouldn't give a damn if I asked him not to. At this time, I was new in the taxi trade and wasn't too sure if I should have asked him to leave. In order to avoid any confrontation with this stubborn bloke, I decided to just drop him off quickly since it was only a two-mile journey.

During the journey, Sean started insulting all taxi drivers and ranted about how they overcharge their customers. He was particularly angry with internet-based taxis, calling the drivers sly con merchants who randomly charge surge prices. I reassured him that there was no surge charge on this journey at least, and that it was a quick route to his house.

He looked at me defensively, waving his fried chicken in the air and dancing with the music.

"You better not take me on a fucking detour around York, I'm local and I know where I am!"

Now I had chicken grease stains all over the back window where Sean had been brushing the drumsticks.

As soon as I pulled up outside his house, I quickly got out of the car to help him so that he wouldn't spill any more curry sauce than what he had already spilt on the seat. As I walked him to his gate, carrying his tub of curry sauce, I cheekily told him that I deserved a tip for my exceptional customer service. Not expecting anything from a guy who had just complained that all taxi drivers were robbers, Sean dipped his hand into his pocket and passed me a handful of change. The money he gave me amounted to just over eighteen pounds.

Despite his initial prejudice, Sean turned out to be one of my best paying customers. Maybe he feels overcharged because he's giving away generous tips like this.

Extortionate Taxi Fares

It is very uncommon for customers to discuss the fare of the journey in an internet-based taxi as they already know it when they order the taxi, and the money is automatically deducted from their personal account. During a busy night, when there is an increased demand of taxis, there is a surge on the fares. Sometimes, when customers are drunk and not paying attention, they could be charged six times the normal fare. A journey that would normally only cost twenty pounds could surprise you with a hundred and twenty pound bill if you're not careful.

Last winter, we had very heavy snowfall on a Saturday night. I remember another taxi driver posted his invoice on our WhatsApp group of twelve hundred pounds for driving a customer from Leeds to London. During snowy weather, a lot of people don't have a choice but to pay the extortionate charges in a desperate attempt to get home.

The surge was especially ridiculous because many drivers had abandoned their cars due to the higher risks of driving on the road, hence the very attractive reward for those who were willing to take that risk. I witnessed approximately six accidents in total that night. People don't realise how severely your driving can be affected in dangerous conditions. You could be the best driver in the world, but you cannot guarantee that someone else won't crash into you.

The Dark Hole

A fellow cabbie told me that one night he spent a few hours driving around a drug dealer to different locations, making drop-offs. He wasn't bothered about the passenger's business as he was making a decent wage from him and it kept him busy. During the rounds, the drug dealer asked the driver to take him home as he needed to collect some more goods.

Whilst the cabbie was waiting outside his house, three vehicles full of male passengers pulled up. They parked on all three sides of the taxi, trapping the car completely. At first, the taxi driver thought these were local drug dealing competitors. He felt like it was his last day on Earth, and desperately wished he was just doing his regular job driving around non-criminal folk.

As soon as the vehicles pulled up, the men jumped out; there must have been about twelve in total. Most of them ran towards the house and a few stayed outside. The driver was approached by one of them, as he waved a CID badge at him through the window.

He identified himself as part of the Police Drugs Squad and told the driver to get out of the car, keeping his hands where they can be seen. After the cabbie got out, he was told to empty his pockets and to inform the police immediately if he was carrying anything illegal. Petrified, the driver took out the half gram of weed he had in his wallet and handed it over straight away.

The cabbie was escorted into the drug dealer's house where they had already handcuffed his passenger against the floor. At this point, the police sniffer dogs had arrived too. The whole house was being searched from top to bottom, including the garden and taxi vehicle. The cabbie had to remain in the house whilst his car was stripped and searched by the police.

The cabbie was taken into the kitchen and advised to follow standard procedure. To make the entire night even more surreal and traumatising, he was asked to pull his trousers down, bend over and spread his butt cheeks so that the police officer could check if he was hiding anything up his backside.

He could see four police officers having a quiet discussion in the garden. Then, one of them walked into the house and pulled the drug dealer from the floor, making him stand upright. This officer told the dealer that they know he has been selling drugs as they have seen the local heroin addicts purchase wraps from him on numerous occasions.

The police officer informed the dealer that although they haven't found anything on this occasion, this should be a huge warning for him unless he would like to end up in prison. The dealer let out a sigh of relief, considering himself lucky this time.

Suddenly, another police officer walked in from the back garden with cartons of Ribena juice that were full of heroin wraps. Their whole attitude changed as they grabbed the dealer and slammed him back down to the ground again. They were shouting at him, telling him that he would be going to prison for a long time. The cabbie realised that the police officers were playing with the dealer by telling him that they didn't find anything, even though they had.

The police were very pleased with their drugs bust, especially one of the officers as it was his last day of work before retirement and it ended with a successful arrest. Due to the magnitude of the heavy drugs found at the house, in comparison to the small amount of weed that was just enough for one spliff, the police officers simply confiscated the cannabis from the cabbie and let him go with a warning.

Organised Taxi Criminal Gang

A young man was waiting outside a busy club at midnight, looking extremely distraught. He was going home early, compared to many people who usually start their night at that time, so I asked him why he was leaving the club early. Apparently, Tom had just received a call from his housemate who had told him that their house had been robbed and someone had stolen their gaming consoles, laptops and televisions.

Tom said that it was the second time he had been robbed during his three years in Leeds, and that it was a common occurrence in student areas. Slightly drunk still, he was crying throughout the journey because he needed his laptop to finish his assignments. He was working full-time at McDonalds to make ends meet so couldn't afford another laptop. And he couldn't ask his parents since they had already paid for the one that had just been stolen after he was robbed the first time. Luckily his work was saved on a memory stick, so at least there was that.

During my time as a taxi driver, I have picked up many people who have been victims of house robberies. Since it is common knowledge that students own electronic devices, they are easy targets for the black market. Not many landlords invest in security alarms anymore because of the nuisance that drunken students cause when they get home in the middle of the night, having forgotten the pass codes and therefore accidentally setting the alarms off and waking up the whole street.

Interestingly enough, I have heard from numerous passengers that they have been robbed when they were on a night out with all of their housemates. The common suspicion is that drivers from a specific taxi firm alert their partners in crime to target these unattended properties, which they know about because of picking up the residents.

The police have launched an ongoing investigation into this organised crime and it should be easy enough for them to check the taxi firm's records and find a correlation between the drivers who picked up the students from the specific properties that have been robbed. Hopefully, they can find culprits from there. It is a very cunning way to exploit students, although it is an absolute disgrace.

Walking Taller

On a frosty Thursday night, I was waiting outside a customer's house. There had been some snowfall earlier which had turned into ice, and the smooth Yorkshire stone pavement became extremely slippery during winter. I watched from my side mirror as the customer walked out of her garden, bravely wearing a dress with four inches on her heels.

As soon as she set foot on the stone paving, she lost her balance and collapsed onto the ground. The sound of the crash was so loud that I was convinced she had broken many bones and would either need to be taken to the hospital or to have an ambulance called.

Immediately, I moved to get out of the car to help her, but by the time I opened the car door, she was up in a flash and said she was perfectly fine. She assured me that there was no need to help her and to carry on with the journey to town as planned. Either she was made of steel, or she had made up her mind that, whether she's dead or alive, she would be going clubbing that night.

Wearing high heels on a night out can be life-threatening if you're not careful, and so often I see girls lose their balance and fall over. These women will sprain their ankles or bang their head and spend the rest of their night at the hospital. Watching women struggle in uncomfortable high heels and willingly suffer the excruciating pain is a global unsolved mystery.

For a lot of women, comfort comes second to appearance. One passenger told me that she has ten different heels in her collection and each pair hurts a different part of her feet. She makes her choice of heels by deciding which pain she wants to endure for the rest of the night. You always hear the sigh of relief when women take their shoes off as soon as they get into a taxi at the end of their night.

Interestingly enough, other Europeans such as the Italians and Spanish are often surprised at the British night culture. They discuss their struggle to understand the fun in going out and not wearing much in cold weather. I've observed that Europeans will always wear a coat and jeans if they're out in the winter, and the cultural differences are surprising.

I once collected two ladies that wanted to go to a hotel that was only one block away, across the road. They didn't want to walk because of their high heels. So, I had to go along the one-way loop system, travelling one and a half miles to drop the girls off across the road because their feet were hurting. At that point, it is time to consider other footwear.

Going out has become an extreme sport.

Cracked Up

As a child, I was always taught to wait for the green man before crossing the road. Cars were always considered to have priority on the roads, but now it's different. People consider the road to be no different than the pavement and some even believe that it's the driver's responsibility to stop for them. During busy city nights, they will see you coming and still step out into the road. What if I was a crazy person on a homicidal rampage?

Why trust drivers that are strangers to you? Not everyone is paying attention whilst they are driving, so if you expect others to watch out for you every time you cross in busy traffic then I wish you the best of luck in your game of Russian roulette. The people who are gazing at their mobile phones or listening to music, completely in a world of their own, are basically toying with their own lives.

One Friday night, a drunken guy fell into the road and smashed his head against the windscreen of a taxi parked in front of my car. The pedestrian fell to the floor and was bleeding from the right side of his forehead as he lay in front of the car, blocking traffic.

The injured man's girlfriend began screaming at the cabbie, when it was no fault of his at all. Not only could the driver not work for the rest of the night because of his damaged windscreen, he had to deal with the girlfriend's intoxicated rage. She further escalated the situation by kicking and denting the side of his car.

Luckily the police are always around the main city streets on busy nights, and quickly defused the row. The city centre has multiple cameras in operation, so these matters get settled easily. In a situation such as this, when the collision is with a pedestrian, the insurance companies usually favour the pedestrians, but the taxi driver's dash cam helped resolve this. Regardless, the damage had been done, both to the man's head and the driver's windscreen, and both nights were ruined.

Through the Wall

I was driving through Calverley, a quiet village on the outskirts of Leeds, when I noticed a taxi that had crashed through a stone wall into the field and landed upside down. The front of the car was completely damaged and the roof was crushed. I parked up, along with another two taxi drivers, to assist the driver and anyone else in the car.

I climbed down into the field, which was a four-foot drop from the roadside. The driver was already outside of his car as he apprehended the drunken passenger on the floor who was trying to get away. It turned out that the passenger was sat in the front seat and for reasons unknown, he grabbed the steering wheel and pulled it to the left which forced the car through the wall and into the field below. The story was inexplicable.

The damage had been done as the vehicle was written off. The driver had suffered the loss of his car as well as a loss of earnings and had to spend the rest of the Saturday night liaising with the police and writing up a report; all because his customer had behaved recklessly.

Drunk Vegans

Drunk vegans must be my favourite passengers for entertainment and conversation. They often discuss their lifestyle choices and share various convincing reasons to not eat meat, to the extent that you genuinely feel guilty about your diet. Before I met vegans in my taxi, my perception of the general community was that they are strong minded people who control their desires due to genuine ethical reasons about the bad treatment of animals.

As I mentioned earlier, people are more honest when they are drunk. Well, they also have less morals. When it comes to vegans, some of them are notorious for treating themselves to a meaty McDonalds after a night out. It's probably the only time when they struggle to control their desire for meat and their concern for animal cruelty temporarily disappears. Until the next morning, of course, when they have sobered up and return to veganism again.

One drunken passenger was talking about how she doesn't

even allow her children to eat eggs, enforcing her vegan lifestyle onto the family. But a few minutes later, she confessed to her friend that she had a cheeky bacon sandwich with her brother as a one-off breakfast treat from him. Now, that sounds like a freegan to me.

I've also had a vegan in the car with a donner kebab, drunk of course, whilst still maintaining a serious conversation about how important it is to be a vegan with his friends. He suffered a hell of allot of verbal abuse from his mates as they tried to snatch his kebab from him, but this die-hard vegan was not going to give up his meat that night. He probably needed this quick fix to be able to sustain his vegan lifestyle on a daily basis. It's a bit like having a nicotine patch and telling everyone that they should stop smoking because it's bad for you.

These fake vegans should be named and shamed, and perhaps even barred from any kind of vegan society. Since I have been in the taxi trade, and due to those that cheat whilst preaching animal cruelty, I can't take vegans seriously anymore. Although I appreciate and understand the health benefits of veganism and have been inspired to eat less red meat myself, I can't stand hypocrites. I'm sure there are many that honour their belief seriously.

Thirsty?

Talking about freegans after a night out, a group of students arranged an eight-seater taxi to get back home in the early hours of the morning. One of the students, Charlie, was dehydrated and desperately needed some water to clear his throat. Coincidentally, there was an open can of cola in the back of the taxi that belonged to a previous passenger.

Drunken Charlie couldn't believe his luck, enthusiastically taking the can to quench his thirst. Unfortunately it was too late when he realised that the can was full not with cola, but with someone's vomit. Charlie, along with three of his friends, threw up during the aftermath of Charlie's nightmare. This was, by far, his worst ever night out. A night to remember.

On the other hand, some people don't mind the taste of vomit. Paul was a student at York University, and was struggling to get a taxi after a night out because his clothes were covered in vomit. He even tried to convince a taxi driver that it was just the remains of a pizza he had ate earlier.

Desperate to prove it was food, he started eating bits of the vomit from his shirt. But the driver still wasn't convinced, which alone says a lot about taxi drivers' experiences with drunken customers. Running out of ideas, and probably even more disgusted with himself, Paul had to walk home that night.

Near Death

Mark was travelling back from York to Leeds early in the morning. During the journey, both Mark and the driver fell asleep on the highway and the car drifted to the right into the oncoming lane. Neither one of them had realised until the vehicle felt the rough rubble of the edge of the road. This awakened the passenger who screamed in horror, alerting the driver who then quickly managed to recover back into the left lane.

Luckily, the roads were quiet at that time of the day and so there was no oncoming traffic. Otherwise, the situation could have been catastrophic. Mark made sure that the driver had both front windows down for the rest of the journey, even though it was freezing.

Mark was angry with the driver but kept his cool as he just wanted to get home alive. He offered to buy the driver a coffee from the service station, but he refused, assuring Mark that he was fine and that this hadn't ever happened before.

Looking back at the encounter, and considering the seriousness of the incident, Mark felt that he should have reported the driver for putting people's lives at risk.

Brazilian Driver

When Sam arrived in Brazil, he got into a cab that stunk of cannabis. The driver was completely stoned out of his head. At first, Sam didn't consider it to be an issue as he thought the driver may be used to smoking cannabis whilst working. However, ten minutes into the ride from the airport to the hotel, the cab driver dozed off at the traffic lights.

Sam shook his shoulders in an attempt to wake him up, whilst the traffic behind were honking at him to move. He reached closer to wake the cabbie and noticed an open can of beer trapped between his legs as well. Suddenly, the cabbie opened his eyes and sped off quickly whilst reassuring Sam.

"Don't worry, everything OK."

"Everything alright my ass, you fell asleep!"

Sam desperately wanted to get to the hotel but was losing confidence in his driver who was both drunk and high. He was debating whether to get another taxi, but eventually the driver delivered Sam to his hotel. He laughed at Sam as though he was the unreasonable one for overreacting, ignoring the fact that he himself was driving under influence. Things are unbelievably different in other countries.

Road Rage

Sometime in winter, Mike was out with his girlfriend in Manchester on a weeknight. It was approximately three a.m. when they caught a cab to go home. On their way, another taxi driver cut into the lane in front of them, forcing their driver to brake fairly hard. This enraged their driver, who then rushed to catch up with the other taxi at the traffic lights. He rolled his window down and began swearing at the other driver in a foreign language.

Their driver got out and walked over to the other taxi driver, who had also opened his door, and began punching him in the face, Suddenly, a fight broke out on the road as they struggled and ripped each other's shirts. Mike and his girlfriend were sitting there in shock and confusion and they just wanted to get home.

The drivers eventually split up after five minutes of struggling due to the cars horning from the built-up traffic behind them. They got back into their taxis, but this wasn't the end. Lui's driver was now driving at seventy mph in a thirty-mph zone, trying to catch up for another fight.

Mike's girlfriend was petrified, screaming for the driver to stop as she wanted to get out of the car. The driver was so full of rage that he was completely oblivious to his passengers. Mike asked the driver how the situation had gotten this bad, and the driver explained: "He swore at my mother."

After begging for him to forget about it, they managed to convince him to get back on route to the couple's house.

The Great Chase

Two students caught a taxi from a club on a Friday night in Leeds. The cabbie was driving recklessly, to the point that the students thought he was drunk. He ran through the first three red traffic lights, which instantly caught the attention of the police who patrol on weekend nights.

The chase was now on. The driver sped through the city centre in a poor attempt of losing the police. Both of the students were begging the driver to slow down but he didn't want to get stopped. Eventually, he realised he wasn't going to get away from the police and they caught up.

As soon as he parked up, the police pulled him out of the car and handcuffed him. He was in tears, crying and begging the police to let him go because he would lose his taxi badge and it was his only form of livelihood. Another police car arrived, collected the taxi and impounded it, which would've cost him three hundred pounds to retrieve.

The driver was sat in the back of the police car, handcuffed and whimpering with snot running down his lips. The students couldn't believe that it was the same guy who had just been acting tough as though he was driving a getaway car. The police promised the boys that they would arrange a lift for them, but alas this never happened. At least they had some excitement; being chased by the police.

He's lost the plot

Two students caught a taxi from near their university campus. They were performing at a local social club and caught a cab because of their heavy music equipment. Whilst en route, a cyclist collided with the taxi and scraped the side of his car.

The driver immediately stopped the car and jumped out to chase the cyclist. The car was still running, and the driver began running as well and was nowhere to be seen for the next twenty minutes.

The guys couldn't wait any longer as they were now getting late for the gig. Eventually, they decided to call for another cab and that's when I arrived on the scene. I helped them take everything out of the other taxi's boot, and we left the car abandoned with the engine still running.

This is a special kind of stupidity, as the scratch on the car is a small repair cost compared to the total cost of the vehicle if it were stolen. One man's loss is another man's gain; in this case, that's mine.

Weird Customer

A fellow taxi driver told me about his bizarre passenger that had booked a taxi to go nowhere. All he wanted was to be driven on a cobbled road because apparently, he found it very soothing.

So, they drove up and down the cobbled road for about ten minutes. The driver observed that the passenger had his eyes closed, as though he was receiving a Chinese massage from the bumps.

Eventually, the passenger felt satisfied enough and requested to be taken back home. A slightly odd but easy enough job for the driver.

No Ambulance

A fellow cabbie had a male customer sitting in the back of his car that was clearly uncomfortable. He was constantly grimacing, complaining that he was in a lot of pain. Hovering above his seat, he held onto the headrest in front of him to keep himself upright.

The passenger's bizarre behaviour continued as they headed to the accident and emergency department at the hospital. The driver grew curious and asked the passenger if he was alright.

"I will be when I get this piece of cucumber out of my backside!"

It turned out that this bloke had plenty of free time on his hands and decided to have a bit of play around his rear end with a cucumber. Somehow, he lost balance and snapped the piece of cucumber in half. The unfortunate half slipped back into his backside, like a vacuum effect, and got lodged.

Struggling to get the piece of vegetable out, he had called for an ambulance, but they insisted that his situation wasn't severe enough and he should make his way to the hospital. The driver felt shivers down his spine and couldn't bear to imagine the pain that the passenger was experiencing.

I shared this story with another passenger that was a nurse. She told me that it was disturbingly common for people to end up in hospital with all types of items stuck in their buttocks. Sometimes it wasn't even sexual or deliberate. Many people would slip in the bath and land with unfortunate precision onto a shampoo bottle. Once, this nurse had a patient who came into the hospital with a toilet brush stuck. I guess he didn't get the memo: better out than in.

Sleeping Beauty

On the night of the MOBO Awards event in Leeds, I picked up a passenger who happened to be a world-famous DJ from Nigeria. DJ Obi was a big name in Nigeria's music industry, and he was considered a national icon.

He also held the Guinness World Record for playing music for eight days straight, without sleep. At first, I thought he was just telling lies. I couldn't comprehend how someone could stay awake for that many hours. I can't even drive the taxi through the night without a coffee.

In order to achieve the record, he had to follow strict guidelines: he was allowed one five-minute break every hour, and a one-hour break every twelve hours. The competition required at least one person dancing at all times and he wasn't allowed to repeat a song within four hours of playing it. During the whole time, there was the concern of being disqualified if he accidentally fell asleep.

He also mentioned that his father was a famous media

professional, but he died in a plane crash a couple of years ago. His legacy lives strong through his successful son, DJ Obi.

The Racist Old Man

During an evening shift in the summer, I received a job from a village in the north of Leeds. It was a grand, beautiful country manor, with an elderly couple waiting outside. They had come to visit their son for an evening meal. The son helped the frail mother into the car, and she sat behind me whilst the old man sat next to her.

The old man was highly intoxicated, which was clear from his slurred speech when I greeted him. Not even two minutes into the journey, he commenced his racist rant, loud and bold.

"Wherever you Asians go, you do nothing but cause trouble and I'm absolutely sick of you!"

I was speechless since this was my first encounter with a racist person, especially in my own car, so it came as quite a shock. But for some reason, I stayed calm and was more interested in why he felt the way that he did. I wanted to engage in a conversation with him.

"You lot have come over here and done nothing!"

I disagreed with this point and proudly informed him that my grandfather was in the British army under the British rule in India and came over to the U.K. after the Second World War. My parents came over here in the sixties, and my father worked long hours in steel factories in Leeds until he scolded his foot and could no longer work. I explained to the old man that I was born in this country and had never had a day off since I started working. I'd like to believe that we are hard-working and peaceful, bringing culture into British society since the national dish is curry after all.

This old man wasn't having any of it and carried on blaring about all the terrorist attacks. He emphasised how ISIS are the root of all evil. I tried to explain that Muslims were the biggest victims of terrorism since ISIS had killed more Muslims than anyone else.

He ignored this remark and changed the subject to Eastern Europeans. In the same effect, he hurled abuse about them coming over here and questioned what was wrong with their own countries. I explained that my parents were invited as economic migrants to help develop the country. He went silent for a few minutes, either pondering on my defence or preparing his attack, but his arrogance refused to let him back down, so he continued.

At this point in the journey, I realised this conversation was not going to progress well, so I decided to remain silent for the rest of it. I didn't want to stop the car and force them to leave since we were driving through eerie country lanes and the couple were easily in their early eighties. It certainly wasn't fair on the silent old lady, and I felt sorry for her that she had to deal with this raving lunatic.

He was a hot-headed person, clear from his face that was as red and hot as a glowing light bulb. He probably got himself into terrible situations by opening his mouth before putting his brain into gear.

Then, since he was a drunken mess, he took a complete turn in conversation and started bragging about his wealth. He said that, although he wasn't intelligent like me, at least he had money – in fact, he had too much money -and didn't give a damn about what people thought of him. I remained silent and figured that he was trying to provoke me, any way that he could.

I also realised that besides his drinking limit, the old man had passed his age of reasoning as well. Either way, we were not going to have a mature conversation tonight since he was on fire and would remain alight, with no chance of sobering up during this journey. I'd better shut up and let him rant and rave.

We finally reached his grand mansion, clearly boasting his wealth. When he got out of the car, he slammed the car door. I could tell that my lack of response had made him angrier, although I don't think it takes much to wind up people of his calibre.

This was my first racist encounter and when I look back at the journey, I think I handled the situation with dignity. Maybe if he was on his own then he would have been walking along the Yorkshire country lanes in the dark and early hours. But lucky for him, his wife saved him from being thrown out of the car and I just took him with a pinch of salt.

I believe that there are no more racist people in the U.K. than anywhere else in the world; it's just a sad reality. But I also believe that diversity is the core of British values, which is only possible from the different races and cultures of those that live here. I feel extremely blessed and grateful to be part of this great country, and no grumpy old man can take that away from me.

South African Passenger

It was a lucrative working day during the national train strike since more people were booking taxis for longer journeys. My passenger Jack was travelling to Huddersfield from Leeds. He had a foreign accent, which was South African, and had only been living in the UK for the past two years. Jack decided to tell me his story.

Jack's parents have always lived in South Africa and recently had their land confiscated from them. They live in a remote part of Africa where they were threatened with machetes and forced to give up all of their assets that they had spent their lives building together.

To survive, Jack's parents made a deal with the people who had taken their livelihood. They arranged to rent the land that had been in their family for centuries until now, whilst farming and selling tobacco leaves to sustain their livelihoods.

According to Jack, the rest of his family and friends are in the same predicament of renting their confiscated property and making a living from growing tobacco leaves. Allot of the younger generation have left for a better standard of living in Australia, New Zealand, Canada and the U.K.

Now, he has relatives scattered all over the world due to the political instability in South Africa. There was a time that they all lived near enough to enjoy their evenings together, but that would never happen again. Instead, they rely on social media networks to regularly stay in touch. Jack and his family never imagined that they would have to leave their home country.

He also mentioned a tragedy regarding his aunt's husband. As common in South Africa, there are many cases of robberies and violence. Stood outside his own house, his aunt's husband was shot in the head by a group of looters. His family witnessed this horrific act happening before their eyes whilst they were sat in their new car, ready to go out for a family dinner. Not long after this traumatic event, his wife and children migrated to Australia.

Jack was much happier living in the U.K. and came across as a strong and confident person. He wanted to pursue his dreams and build a life with his wife and two-year-old son. He was also trying for his parents to move here, since they are getting old and there is no one to look after them in South Africa. They hope to spend the rest of their days with Jack and his family living in Yorkshire.

Irish Robbie

had an Irish customer who described an experience he had in a cab in Ireland. The cabbie was obsessed with wanting to know whether the passenger was a Catholic or a Protestant. The passenger knew that if he gave the wrong answer, then he many never reach his destination. It was a significant issue in Ireland. Choosing to play it safe, he told the driver that he was Jewish. The driver didn't converse with him after that, but at least he got to where he wanted to go in peace.

Taxi Driver Anonymous

One evening, three young student girls caught a taxi from the Tesco supermarket car park heading back to their halls of residence with their weekly shopping. The driver politely asked if they could wait for a few minutes, as his boss was arriving to collect the weekly taxi base rent. Fifteen long minutes later, a dodgy black VW Golf pulled up alongside their driver, with two young guys sat in the front.

The girls remained in the dark as they all began talking in some foreign language. Then, disguised as a hand shake, the taxi driver reached over to give the guy some money, and in the same exchange they handed him a bag of weed. The girls realised what had happened due to the unmistakable odour of cannabis which immediately polluted the car.

There was no way that the driver could hide that he had just bought some fresh bud. The rest of the journey was awkward to say the least, as the girls were aware that he had lied about paying his weekly rent, and really he had made the girls wait for his fix. Now embarrassed, he was driving like a lunatic and probably couldn't wait to get the girls out of the car – or to roll up a joint.

The girls rightfully noted his badge number and reported him to the police. It served him right for being a selfish druggy.

Part-time Dealer, Part-time Driver

A group of students from Leeds went out clubbing in Newcastle one weekend, meeting up with some friends that study there. That night when they caught a cab, they were under the impression that taxi drivers in Newcastle were a great source for drugs. They asked the cabbie if he could get them some weed, but instead he advised them that weed is a waste of money and just affects people's health. His fatherly advice continued, as he suggested that his friend sold good quality cocaine that he can get hold of easily if they were interested in having a real buzz. The boys kindly declined the offer and went on to ask someone at the club instead.

On another night, the same group of boys were on their way home after a night out in Leeds city centre. Recklessly, the taxi driver decided to snort a quick line of cocaine off the dashboard. He offered for the boys to join in and test the goods out, before giving them his mobile number for future reference. This time, the boys went for it and finished their night on a real high.

The Ex-CID Passenger

It was a Sunday afternoon when an unusually tall male, probably six and a half feet, jumped into the front seat of my car and kindly asked if he could pull the seat back to get comfortable. Tom was a former policeman, now retired as a CID officer, and shared some of the thrilling experiences from his career in law enforcement.

He recounted the time that he dined at a Chinese restaurant with his work colleagues. The restaurant used to be a working men's club but had since turned into a modern Chinese restaurant with a seating capacity of approximately a hundred and fifty people. On the night that they were there, the restaurant was well-staffed, with almost ten waiters on the restaurant floor and at the bar.

The guys had a pleasant meal with some beverages and stayed there for approximately two and a half hours. During this time, they found it suspicious that they were the only table in the entire restaurant, considering the number of seats, as well as the staff. It would be quite difficult for the business to still exist if this was the state it was in on a weekend. As intellectual CID agents, it didn't take them very long to reach the conclusion that there may be a cannabis farm in the basement.

After they left the restaurant, they arranged for a helicopter to fly over the building at night when the restaurant was closed in order to detect any unusual heat radiation. Cannabis farms require allot of electricity for heating and lighting in order to create a suitable climate for the plants to grow properly. As suspected, the building lit up like a Christmas tree on the heat radar, indicating some unusual activity.

A few days later, a raid was carried out on the building and found the whole basement was full of cannabis plants, covering three thousand square feet and worth nearly a million pounds in street value. Caught red-handed, thirteen illegal Chinese immigrants that were sleeping in rooms loaded with mattresses were arrested.

Tom also mentioned that when the roofs of houses are covered in snow during the winter, you may come across a house which stands out in the street because there is no snow on the roof. The chances are that the residents are growing cannabis in the attic or loft, because only the heat from the lighting would melt the snow. The roof is left bare and exposed, just as the criminal activity. If you notice anything like that on your street, then you know what your neighbours are up to – and you may have found a convenient dealer.

The Bus Stop Woman

One morning, I was waiting outside a medical centre for a customer to arrive. There was no one else on the road except for a woman in her mid-forties, waiting at the bus stop across the road. I looked over at her to get her attention and when she noticed, she turned away. A clear indication to me that she had not ordered a taxi. As required by the taxi firm, I only have to wait for five minutes and then I am allowed to cancel the job. However, I decided to call the customer in case she was waiting inside the medical centre and hadn't realised that her cab had arrived.

Whilst I was calling the customer, I noticed that the lady at the bus stop had taken her phone out of her handbag and placed it next to her ear. To my surprise, she turned out to be the passenger. Cindy sounded angry over the phone, complaining that I didn't drive over to the bus stop to pick her up.

I told her that when I looked at her, she turned away and didn't even wave at me to indicate that she was the customer.

How was I supposed to know? This arrogant woman didn't have the common sense to walk over and get into a taxi that was clearly there for her. Instead, she remained at the bus stop and expected me to use my psychic skills to know that she was the passenger.

Begrudgingly, I decided to pull up nearer to her to take her home. In hindsight I should have just cancelled the job since she was dismissive of anything I had to say.

'You could have easily checked my car's registration number on the app to confirm I was your driver?'

In response to this, she told me that I was patronising her and threatened to file a complaint for my unprofessional behaviour. She was full of anger and somehow, everything was my fault. I completely switched myself off during the rest of the journey and ignored whatever she was muttering under her breath.

Maybe she realised that it was her fault but couldn't bring herself to admit it. On arrival, I parked outside her house without saying a word and expected her to slam the car door like the child she was behaving as. My predication was spot on.

The Posh Guy from Harrogate

It was around Christmas time when I picked up John after his festive work night out in Leeds, heading to Harrogate. During the journey, John had his hands on his stomach whilst retching, as if his food was trying to come back up. I immediately stopped the car, asking him if he was alright or if he needed to get out of the car to vomit.

Ever since my first vomit ordeal with Sarah, I always kept carrier bags in the glove compartment, a gesture of common sense that customers appreciate. If I think that a passenger is not feeling right, I would either pass the bag or even stop the car for the customer to step outside. So, I offered him one of my carrier bags just in case he needed to puke during the journey. John insisted that I should carry on with the journey to Harrogate, accusing me of overreacting.

Not long after this, I heard him throw up. I pulled over again.

"Why didn't you just say? I told you I had bags in the car, and you could have told me to stop the car too!"

Arrogantly, John didn't want to admit that he had a problem. Instead, he tried to hold his vomit in his mouth, which ended up shooting down his sleeves and all over his jacket. I looked at this fool in absolute disgust and asked him if he wanted to step out of the car to finish throwing up.

Startled and still drunk, he sat there staring at me sheepishly like a child. In fact, it's probably unfair to compare this guy to a child, since even children are more communicative.

John, a respectably dressed, well-spoken and qualified architect, who appeared to be the sort of person who uses his brain quite often, sadly didn't want to admit that he had an upset stomach. Apparently, that is more humiliating than vomiting over his expensive clothes.

Refusing to leave the car, he insisted that he didn't need to vomit anymore but reluctantly accepted the plastic bag as a precaution for the rest of the journey. On route to Harrogate, there was a twenty-four hour petrol station, so I suggested for him to go in and clean himself up to some extent, but again he refused.

At this point, I was bewildered. I couldn't believe this guy – he didn't even feel the need to clean himself after such an undignified accident! He was so filled with pride that he didn't want to show the public what a spectacle he had made of himself, stinking of booze and vomit which was all over his flashy suit.

Throughout the journey to his house, he was apologising repeatedly – apart from when he paused to puke in the bag -but I remained silent. I felt that my silence would teach this arrogant man a lesson. Even though it was freezing outside, I had put all four windows down to allow plenty of fresh air in the car, which really only helped dry the vomit into his clothes.

Once we arrived at John's beautiful detached property outside of Harrogate, he was kind enough to give me a tip of twenty pounds for the inconvenience. This somewhat softened the blow, and I gladly accepted and thanked him for not making a mess in the car.

However, before John left, he had the courage to ask me if the bag of vomit could remain in the car. I burst out laughing, unable to control my disbelief that he would even suggest such a ridiculous thing.

"You take that bag with you, my friend. It's your puke not mine."

The cheek of this man was unbelievable. He wanted me to dispose of his bag on my way back to Leeds. He didn't want to take the smell into his house, even though the stench would follow him anyway, but had no problem leaving it with me. I looked at him incredulously and repeated myself.

"Look, don't be silly – you take your shit with you. I am disgusted that you want me to dispose of your bag. You should be grateful that I even had a bag for you to use, and still managed to take you home."

I couldn't help but laugh at his courage. Luckily the car had survived his antics, although I couldn't say the same for his clothes. His request was probably out of fear of his wife finding out what a mess he had been. I'm sure she would be unimpressed regardless when he went inside. Looks like Mr. Perfect screwed up today.

Arrogance is a very expensive attribute.

Often, I will observe the customers before they get into the car to see how drunk they are. The thing is, I don't mind stopping the car as long as people tell me in advance that they're feeling sick. But with experience, you know that there's likely going to be some problems if someone is being carried by their friends to even get into the car.

Most of the time, people are coherent enough to be able to successfully use the taxi phone app in the first place. The app works like an automated filter system, allowing you to only attract customers who are at least somewhat in control of their senses.

On one encounter, it was a cold winter's night with the temperature at minus one, I picked up two guys. At first, they were speaking well and showed no signs of being drunk. It wasn't until one of the guys quickly wound the back window down, stuck his head out of the moving car and released his vomit onto the road, that I realised how hammered they were.

I was grateful to see a customer thinking quickly for once, saving me from the nightmare of a mess inside the car. But my gratitude didn't last long when my next customers alerted me about the frozen vomit along the back door and the rear wing panel. This time, my luck was in order because this passenger was kind enough to run into his house and get me a kettle of boiled water to wash off the tragedy.

Abducted Driver

Etched into his memory, Leon told me an experience from many years ago when he caught a cab and his driver shared that he had been abducted before. Apparently, Leon's driver had been abducted by some aliens during his childhood and since then, they have been following him.

Then, suddenly and ominously, the cabbie said that they were being followed right then because the aliens overheard him speaking about them. He wanted to take a detour to lose the stalking aliens, but Leon informed him that if he changed the route then he doesn't want to continue this journey. The driver clearly had some serious issues, and Leon wasn't interested in any of this nonsense about aliens.

The driver remained serious, describing how the aliens planted a chip inside his body when he was abducted and that he can sometimes still feel a tingling sensation at the back of his head. Sarcastically, Leon asked which battery was in the chip for it to last this long, as his car battery goes flat every month.

The driver ignored Leon and was now on a mission for a quick getaway. Leon realised that he had changed the route and was frustrated with the driver's antics, so he told him to stop the car. As he left, he took the driver's badge number and reported him.

There are two plausible explanations here. He was trying to fool the customer to make extra money through a detour, or he genuinely believed that he was abducted and tormented by aliens, and therefore has mental health issues. To be honest, nowadays it could even be the aftermath of abusing psychedelic substances. Regardless, he needs to be out of the taxi business.

The Conspiracy Theorist

Tim was once sat in a taxi with a driver that was also a part-time conspiracy theorist. The driver was talking passionately about his theory of doomsday. He warned Tim that there could be a meteorite hitting the Earth at any time, which would plunge the world into chaos. It would cause fires, damage infrastructure and lead to a severe shortage of food. This would lead to civil unrest as people became desperate in their search for food.

But not to worry, the driver had a plan. His advice was to stock up on tinned food and store it in a basement. Tim challenged this plan, asking what the plan would be if the meteorite hit his basement with all of this food.

'Then that is a chance that you take. It's the best chance you have.'

Either way, Tim argued, they are doomed for doomsday. 'When it happens, it will affect all of us, so it doesn't matter how many tins you have.'

'But you should still be prepared.'

Tim didn't want to get into an argument over a theory like this. No doubt, this driver had conveniently hidden meat tins and dried fruit around his house. Tim thanked the driver, shaking his hand, and left the taxi with a warning about the end of the world.

Street in Bloom

was parked up in a terraced street, waiting for Jenny who was my customer. There are many streets like this in Leeds, all built over a hundred years ago. However, this street was especially mesmerising since each house had the same colour plant pot placed on the side of the entrance.

There was one property that attracted my attention with its various flower pots on display. A lady in her late fifties stepped out of this house to water her plants, as well as her neighbour's plants, which indicated a close-knit neighbourhood.

Eventually my customers came out of the house next door to the old lady, exchanged some friendly words with her and then hurried into the cab. I complimented their colourful street, telling Jenny and her partner how beautiful and vibrant the scene looked in the sunshine.

The customers explained that all of the plant pots in the street belonged to the old lady. Everyday, whilst she is watering the plants pots, she would peep through the neighbour's windows.

She also came out under the disguise of tending to the plants whenever any vehicle pulled into the street, just to see what was going on. I guessed that this was why she first appeared when I arrived.

The neighbours despised her intrusiveness. Often when Jenny accidentally dropped something in her home, her neighbour would rush over to ask if everything was alright and to find out exactly what that noise was.

Sometimes, Jenny and her partner won't even open the door if they know it's her. But the old lady was stubborn, repeatedly knocking on the door until someone opened it. The couple were beyond infuriated with her antics and were looking to move elsewhere before they end up strangling her.

Strange Passenger

It was a few hours after midnight on a Thursday when I collected three drunken passengers heading back to their student halls of residence after a night out. One of the guys sat next to me in the front seat and the other in the back with a girl. During the journey, the bloke in front introduced himself to the other guy, both exchanging names. The girl spoke up, puzzled.

"Don't you guys know each other?"

After hearing her question, I stopped the car. I had to make sure that everyone was on the same page before travelling together. I turned around and asked the girl which of the guys she knew, and she confirmed that it was Tom in the front.

But whilst Sarah and Tom knew each other, they both didn't know the third guy sat in the back. Sarah thought Tom knew the guy and Tom thought Sarah knew the guy. They got this impression from his confidence: he jumped into the car and they thought he wanted a lift to the halls. Finally, Tom asked the guy what he was doing in the car.

"You said I could come back with you to your place for the night."

Tom was startled at this response and denied saying anything like that. He asked the guy to get out of the car. However, this strange individual refused to leave the car and insisted that he wanted to go back with Tom and Sarah.

I couldn't believe the stupidity of the whole situation. Why do you want to go back to unknown people's residence when you're not even welcome?

The stranger said he was from Halifax, a small town twenty miles out of Leeds. He wanted somewhere to stay for the night, promising to leave in the morning. Although this invitation was clearly not there, he remained adamant that he wasn't leaving the car.

I sensed that he wasn't foolish, but actually a cunning man, preying on young drunk students to get into their apartments. Regardless, this fare was in Tom's name, so I intervened, looking at the stranger through the rear mirror.

"Come on man, get out of the car! I haven't got time for this nonsense, I have to move on."

Quietly, he moved his head from left to right like a child, indicating that he wasn't going to move. Suddenly, Tom jumped out and ran around the car to the stranger's door. He tried to pull him out of the seat by grabbing his right arm and leg. The bewildered stranger began screaming and shouting "leave me alone, let go of me" as if he was the victim under duress in this situation. I could see this would get messier.

As a taxi driver, I have to remain calm and avoid any confrontation. If this situation escalated, there would not only be a risk of the car getting damaged, but a physical fight would lead to the police getting involved. This could lead to me being suspended whilst a full investigation was carried out by the taxi authorities, which could take months. The days of carrying a baseball bat in the boot for protection are long over.

I convinced Tom to leave him alone and get back in the car with the hope of finding police officers in the city. Not long after, we saw a police van parked on the main street, near one of the clubs. I pulled alongside the van and wound the window down to converse with the police.

Swiftly, as though he had been given a shock, the stranger jumped out of the car. He told Tom that he hates "southern bastards" and promised to "crack Tom's head open" if he ever saw him again. Slamming the car door, the guy sprinted away before the police could intervene.

We all shared a sigh of relief for getting rid of him. On Tom's cue, we began laughing at the insanity of some people. But luckily no one fell for his act, and on a serious note, he could have even robbed the place whilst they were asleep.

One Dog at a Time

One afternoon, I was parked in an affluent area in North Yorkshire waiting for a customer. I couldn't help but notice the two beautifully groomed dogs standing guard behind the gates of the house next door to my pickup point.

When my passenger Blake arrived, he told me that the dogs were of a Doberman Pinscher breed. Then, he began to tell me about the time when his neighbour Mark went on holiday for a week and asked Blake to feed the dogs whilst he was away.

Blake agreed to open the front door in the morning and evening to allow both dogs to come out, eat their food and relieve their bowels in the garden. After ten to fifteen minutes of playing around outside in the garden, they would go back in when Blake opened the house door.

Blake was strongly advised not to enter the property under any circumstances. The idea was that the dogs would come in and out themselves, without Blake having to go into the property to shout them. They did a three-day trial run so that the dogs would become more familiar with Blake.

The first morning after the neighbour left, Blake opened the front door and both dogs came running out to have their food. After twenty minutes, they went back into the house as expected. However, later in the evening only one dog came out. Blake shouted for the other dog, since he wasn't allowed to go into the house, but there was no response at all. After waiting for half an hour, Blake was confused and worried, but he sent the first dog back inside.

The next morning, the other dog was still missing. Despite Blake's concern, he had to stick to the rules as they had been given for his safety. For the rest of the week, only one of the dogs came out and Blake was convinced that the second dog must have died after a week with no food or water.

When his neighbour returned from his holiday, Blake immediately informed him of the situation. The neighbour rushed into the house, concerned about his dog's wellbeing. Blake was anxious for some news but didn't receive any. After an hour, the police had arrived and went into the house.

A little while later, the police left the property with a young male who was in an awful state. It turned out that his neighbour's house had been broken into from the side door. The dogs kept the thief in the house for the entire week. They took it in turns to eat their food and empty their bowels. The thief was held captive on the floor, urinating and defecating on the carpet since the loyal dogs would savagely attack him whenever he attempted to move.

Later that evening, both dogs came out to play.

Conclusion

When I embarked upon the journey of writing this book, I was excited to have the opportunity to share my experiences and concerns. Delving into the lives of strangers has been overwhelming. I felt like I had a lot of weight on my shoulders that I needed relief from.

As it so happened, I was travelling out of the city with a female customer who became pleasantly interested in my encounters and listened attentively. Eventually we arrived at her destination, but before she left, she suggested that it would be great if I were to write a book of short stories from my taxi trips.

I agreed it was a good idea, but I was reluctant to take the initial step of collating the stories. I knew I would have to dedicate a lot of hours – hours that could've been spent working – in order to put this book together. Time is literally money in the taxi trade.

For the next few days, I toyed with the idea. I began telling my passengers, with no real intention, that I was going to write a book about my encounters with passengers in the taxi. The response was absolutely thrilling. I had raised a lot of eyebrows and people expressed their interest as they asked for my name, noting it down so they could search for the book when it's completed.

My excitement for writing this book went from zero to hero over the next few days, thanks to the passengers I came across. They had obliterated any ounce of hesitation. I decided that no matter what, this needed to be written. The seed had been planted and there was no going back now.

That's how I started writing a book for the first time in my life. As I wrote everything down, it felt like a miracle was taking form. It particularly helped me have a clear and serious understanding of the effects of alcohol on society.

No matter how important you are in your daily life, whether you're a CEO or a cleaner, if you drink past your limit then there is a good chance you will do something you will regret. Alcohol doesn't differentiate between well-respected people and the regular unknown individual. It's all the same in a drunken state.

It also helped me to learn about the core group of society: today's youth. If parents knew what some of their children got up to at university, they would never let them leave home! A strong academic background doesn't necessarily mean that you won't get influenced by people who abuse cocaine, ketamine, cannabis, along with all the other manufactured hallucinogenic drugs available on the market nowadays. Whoever these eighteen-year olds befriend in the first few weeks at university will greatly influence their behaviour over the next few years.

I came across a great quote that is relevant here:"Show me your friends and I will tell you your future."

Besides raising some genuine concerns about our society, I do hope that you thoroughly enjoyed the stories about the wonderful and colourful human race. Wherever we are residing around the planet, people do the same crazy stuff and hide their little secrets from everyone, except for that special, but temporary, taxi driver friend.

We will get you from A to B – a small trip as part of your incredible life journey. And we are honoured.

Printed in Poland
by Amazon Fulfillment
Poland Sp. z o.o., Wrocław

49100649R00105